Valley
of
Search

Valley of Search

A Personal
Quest
for Truth

by

ANGELA
ANDERSON

ONEWORLD
OXFORD

Valley of Search
A Personal Quest for Truth

Oneworld Publications Ltd
185 Banbury Road
Oxford, OX2 7AR
England

© Angela Anderson 1968, 1990
All rights reserved.
Copyright under Berne Convention
Second revised edition published 1990
by Oneworld Publications

A CIP record for this book is
available from the British Library

Printed and bound in Great Britain by
The Guernsey Press Co. Ltd
Guernsey, Channel Islands

ISBN 1-85168-010-1

'The stages that mark the wayfarer's journey from the abode of dust to the heavenly homeland are said to be seven. Some have called these Seven Valleys, and others, Seven Cities. And they say that until the wayfarer taketh leave of self, and traverseth these stages, he shall never reach the ocean of nearness and union, nor drink of the peerless wine. The first is:

THE VALLEY OF SEARCH

'The Steed of this Valley is patience; without patience the wayfarer on this journey will reach nowhere and attain no goal. Nor should he ever be downhearted; if he strive for a hundred thousand years and yet fail to behold the beauty of the Friend, he should not falter. For those who seek the Ka'bih of "for Us" rejoice in the tidings: "In Our ways will We guide them". In their search, they have stoutly girded up the loins of service, and seek at every moment to journey from the plane of heedlessness into the realm of being. No bond shall hold them back, and no counsel shall deter them.

'It is incumbent on these servants that they cleanse the heart — which is the wellspring of divine treasures — from every marking, and that they turn away from imitation, which is following the traces of their forefathers and sires, and shut the door of friendliness and enmity upon all the people of the earth . . .

'The true seeker hunteth naught but the object of his quest, and the lover hath no desire save union with his beloved. Nor shall the seeker reach his goal unless he sacrifice all things. That is, whatever he hath seen, and heard, and understood, all must he set at naught, that he may enter the realm of the spirit, which is the City of God.'

From *The Seven Valleys of Bahá'u'lláh*.

PART ONE

'The Steed of this
Valley is Patience'

From *The Seven Valleys*

I

'FINISH'

IT WAS ONE OF THE INDONESIAN GIRLS who had spoken. I opened my eyes. It was over, apparently. I could go home.

I looked round the room — the familiar room which had witnessed so much of my struggle for self-awareness over the past three years, but which did not seem familiar now, pervaded by this strange oriental atmosphere. The fifteen other women, also 'beginners', were sitting where they had been half an hour ago — 'not too near together', the Indonesian girl had said when we came in and were spaced several feet apart round the wall. I wondered if they had made any more of the experience than I had.

The chanting had stopped at the word 'Finish' and the half-dozen 'helpers' had gathered together in the centre of the room — a heavily-built and imposing Indonesian woman in a sarong, two young Indonesian girls in Western clothes and three English women. One of the English women detached herself from the group and came over to speak to me. It was Elizabeth — the only familiar person in the room.

Elizabeth was a down-to-earth, matter-of-fact person, and yet she had been taking part in the proceedings as though nothing was untoward. When, about half way through, I had ventured to open my eyes for a moment, there she had been, slowly raising her arms above her head.

The movements and the continuous chanting were all part of the same — the same what? And we who had just sat by — had we been part of it too? Apparently.

I looked round again. It *was* the same room, for there was the photograph over the mantelpiece. It was not because it had been cleared of furniture, and rugs had been placed on the floor, that it seemed strange and oriental, because I had seen it like that many times. It was this *thing* which had come with the Indonesians.

I was not usually attracted by airs of oriental mystery, the only impression I was left with, and if this scene had been enacted anywhere else I would certainly not have come back a second time. But I had had it on good authority that the coming of these Indonesians had great significance, that to 'start the exercise' was the first step in participating in what they had brought, that this 'exercise', though it seemed I had done no exercise, must be persevered with.

It was no wonder that I felt so out of my depth that July evening of 1957 in the dining room of Coombe Springs, an Edwardian mansion standing in seven acres of grounds some seven or eight miles south-west of London, and which for the past twelve years had been used as a centre for the study and practice of human self-development. For it seemed that what was happening now was the very antithesis of everything which usually happened here.

The photograph over the mantelpiece was that of Georges Ivanovitch Gurdjieff. By the time of his death in 1949, Gurdjieff had inspired many pupils with his ideas and methods for developing the powers latent within human beings. It was one of these pupils, J. G. Bennett, who was the Director of the work here.

And demanding work it was too. How often had I struggled to keep my attention from wandering from our exercises, again and again to find I had failed, that my thoughts had become occupied with something quite different, and I must bring myself back to the point I had reached before the dispersion occurred. But *now*, on this occasion, we were told not to direct anything. Time and again had we struggled with our bodies, to make them obedient to our wills, to do what we had intended and not something else quite different. But *this* time we were told to make no move of our own volition.

Here in this very room had I sat on many occasions, in company with maybe fifty, maybe eighty others, and offered observations from which, together, we could gain understanding of the forces which are at play in our lives. Over these three years, from meetings such as these, and from those of our smaller group which met fortnightly, I had become aware of how little control I had over any of my thoughts or actions. And I had realised, also, that others were just as helpless as I was.

All these efforts, all these struggles; to be, to do, to understand. No wonder it was strange to be asked to just let it happen. But the biggest departure from what I had come to consider as the norm here was the fact that in her few words of introduction the Indonesian girl had used the word 'God'.

When Pak Subuh, the founder of the Subud movement, came to England from his home in Java and was invited to make Coombe Springs his headquarters, all but a small minority of the five hundred people who had been going there to take part in the work directed by J. G. Bennett, joined in the practice of the 'Subud exercise'. Thirty at a time, we would enter the temporary building which had been hastily erected in the grounds for the purpose and, closing our eyes, would wait for this 'something' inside us to take over.

Gradually I found that there was something within me that directed my body, and that it was possible to be attentive to this and to follow it. Gentle swaying movements came first, then as I learned not to resist, first my arms moved, and then my feet. There came a day when at the end of the half-hour I found I had landed up in another part of the room, and as time went on I moved about with more and more freedom. Vocal sounds were slower in coming, but eventually I learned not to resist these, also.

In due course it became clear why we were doing it, why it was called an exercise, and what the aim was. The aim was to live one's life according to the Will of God. The exercise was to let go of the reins, so to speak, and let something else take over entirely. Whatever happened, you did not interfere, but let it happen. You practised, for half-an-hour twice a week, this complete surrender. Then maybe there would come a day when you could live your life, not according to your own will, but according to God's Will.

Although, as I drove home that first evening, my only feeling about this 'exercise' was one of disappointment and anticlimax, nevertheless it was a turning point in my life — in fact, not just a turning point, but the great pivotal point in my life.

For this movement from the Far East, known as Subud — an abbreviation of the Sanskrit words Susila Budhi Dharma and usually translated as 'Right living in accordance with the Will of God' — this movement was the means whereby I came to make the biggest decision that anyone can make: the decision to surrender my will to God's Will, and to give my life to Him.

I cannot pin-point any one moment in time when this decision was made, nor can I look to any specific act of dedication. I only know that it was not long before that had become my attitude, that a conscious permanent decision had been made, and that my life since then has consisted in following through the consequences of that decision. What those consequences were to be I could then have had no idea.

II

IT WAS NO ACCIDENT that I came to be numbered among those five hundred people who were attached to Coombe Springs at that time. At least, the long arm of coincidence was stretched so far that only the most cynical could call it so.

I had led a restricted life in my childhood and teens and I had come to long more than anything for freedom. Then at nineteen, with the change of circumstances brought by the end of the war, freedom came and, although I had none of the material comforts to which I had been accustomed, I could come and go with no questions asked, so I had not minded.

This freedom had lasted for two years, and during those years my attention had been caught up in the needs of the moment: work at the office, studying by correspondence course in the evening, preparing for examinations, the busy life of flat-sharing with two other girls, housekeeping in the restricted conditions of the immediate post-war period, adjusting to types of people I had never come across before, in short, *making* a new way of life instead of just fitting into one which was already there. And, in the future, when I had served my apprenticeship, passed my examinations, qualified as a Chartered Accountant . . . all sorts of possibilities would open up.

One day I remember standing waiting for a bus and wondering if this was the way I should be living my life — catching buses, going to the office, and so on, or if life had something quite different to offer, something I was missing. But this was an isolated occurrence, and for the most part I was engulfed in the present, and the next day, the next week, just came and went.

Then at twenty-one, I contracted T.B., and the next four years were spent in hospitals, in bed in my father's house in Scotland, or in a sanatorium. These were waiting years and I was not aware of any problems that a return to health and strength would not solve. In an active life, month follows month with great rapidity, but lying in bed, each day drags slowly by, a week is a long period of time, and a month as much as the mind can encompass. In the beginning, the seriousness of my condition had been kept from me, so I had never adjusted my sights to a long illness; I never looked further than another three months in bed before my convalescence and preparing for entrance into the Promised Land of When-I-Am-Better. But this Promised Land had been like a mirage; whenever I thought I was coming near to it, it would recede again into the distance.

The time came, however, when it did not recede, when the mirage turned out to be a real oasis after all.

Then I was bound to look at life and ask if it was just for this that I had made the wearisome struggle across the desert. For it had not all been waiting; I had been ill enough for it to be a struggle for survival that had pulled me through. Why had I bothered? What was it for? If I had been able to be more mobile, I might have just plunged into activities I imagined were the best the world had to offer, but there was still a danger of the disease flaring up again and caution was necessary. The doctors had prescribed plenty of rest and only a part-time job. I had had time to read and to think.

It was at this time that I heard the name of Gurdjieff. I was looking down the catalogue which my library had sent me one day, and saw a book described as 'an account of the philosophies of Gurdjieff and Ouspensky'. I had never heard of either Gurdjieff or Ouspensky, but the word philosophy probably attracted me because I had enjoyed it at school, and I put that book, *Venture with Ideas* down on my list. In due course it arrived from the library.

This book stirred ideas dormant for many years. I must have been about eleven when the problem of free-will had occurred to me. Out for a walk in the park with whoever was looking after me at the time, I would speculate, 'If I had done such-and-such a thing, how would I know whether I had done it in preference to something else, or because I could have done none other?' I could not find the answer by experiment, because if I said 'I will do that', how could I know whether the decision itself came from choice or compulsion? Maybe, I had supposed, we were all just puppets; our actions, our thoughts, everything, came from some outside source, leaving us only with the illusion of control.

Now, fifteen years later, as I read this book in which Kenneth Walker described P. D. Ouspensky's exposition of Gurdjieff's teachings, something seemed to make sense. According to this teaching, we are not the rational and conscious beings that we like to imagine ourselves to be, but neither are we completely powerless. I liked the feeling of the book and of Ouspensky's detached attitude to his ideas. It was the reader's responsibility to take hold of his words, to experiment with life and to come back with observations. It all seemed very real; Ouspensky had no patience with verbosity, pretensions or prejudice.

The book covered the period from 1923 until Gurdjieff's death in 1949, Ouspensky having died a little earlier. It seemed that that was that. It never occurred to me to wonder what had happened to all those people who had attended the lectures given by Ouspensky in London, where he had come from Russia just after the Russian Revolution, or to ask whether any of this teaching was still going on. But, without attaching any special significance to it, I added another book to my library list — Ouspensky's *In Search of the Miraculous*. A weekend with a friend called Odette provided the next link in the chain. Glancing at the bookshelf in her room, the title of one book caught my eye — *In Search of the Miraculous* by P. D. Ouspensky.

Why should Odette have this particular book, I

wondered. I had long been aware that she attached much importance to some place she visited at weekends, but I had never been particularly curious to find out why. Now it all fell into place — the meetings which Kenneth Walker had described in his book were not just something of the past — even now there were groups studying these ideas and trying to put them into practice. This was the way Odette and her mother and other members of their family were trying to live their lives. Where I had felt indifference, I now felt curiosity. When I got home I wrote to the library, requesting they send me that book next, and in due course the battered copy they had dug up arrived. By the time I had finished it I was more convinced than ever that Gurdjieff's method really got to grips with things. But I could not work alone; I needed the help of other people and of teachers, which I was to find at that place which Odette visited so regularly — Coombe Springs. As a result of her introduction I was invited to visit and see for myself what took place there. It was not long before I also became a regular participant in their activities.

The ideas had attracted me, but what I found at Coombe Springs did not attract me. In 1953 I started to participate in the activities, but it turned out to be a false start. I found myself unable to go for a short time, and felt such a sense of relief that I did not resume them. As time went by I thought less and less about it. Then occurred one of those events which left me in no doubt that a Higher Power was taking a hand in my affairs.

When the weather was fine, a number of the residents of the Guest House in which I was then living could be found sitting on the porch on a Sunday morning. On this particular Sunday there were only two of us: myself and Sally — a woman whom I did not know very well, but with whom I had played bridge occasionally. We were reading the Sunday papers.

There was a review in Sally's paper of some book connected with Gurdjieff's system. She started talking about it, saying that whoever wrote the review did not understand what the book was about. I was surprised, and began to talk to her about Coombe Springs, of my belief in the value of these methods, and my own sense of inadequacy to achieve anything thereby. 'If you do what you can', she said, 'the rest will be given to you.'

I did not see Sally again; the events of her life took her away, and I never heard what became of her, but her words stuck in my mind, for she spoke with great assurance.

'If you do what you can, the rest will be given to you.' It was a promise. Why I should not question Sally's authority to make such a promise I do not know. I accepted her as a 'messenger', on the strength of whose promise I renewed my connection with Coombe Springs.

III

'ALTHOUGH WE MAKE STATEMENTS such as "I do this", "I think that", there is really no entity within us which has the right to say "I". There is only a succession of ephemeral "me"s, each called forth by a different external stimulus, none taking any responsibility for the other's actions.'

This is one of Gurdjieff's fundamental doctrines. However, he also taught that it is possible for a person to develop in himself a 'permanent imperishable I', something which can act on the world instead of being the chance result of forces acting upon it. It was with the aim of developing this 'permanent imperishable I' that we who came to Coombe Springs put ourselves under the direction of J. G. Bennett and his associates and endeavoured to carry out the tasks we were set, both at Coombe Springs and, more important, in our daily lives.

The hypothesis that the unreal 'I' was not one but legion, was something made very clear to me by the circumstances of my life. For it had, since childhood, been lived in many environments, and in each environment I had been a different person. There had been one at my mother's home in London and another at my father's home in Scotland; one at boarding school and later, when I started office life, another again had emerged, and so on. If I had happened to find myself in the presence of two people from different 'lives', I had been thrown into hopeless confusion, not knowing whom I was meant to be.

To be always one and the same. It was easy to see that this was important, and to fight the 'false front' necessary. The chief factor in its formation was the opinions of other people. If one had no autonomy, but existed only in the opinions of others, then one was completely dependent on them. At Coombe Springs we aimed to become free of this.

Before coming to Coombe Springs I had thought I was abnormal; preoccupied with trying to give the appearance of normality, so that no one would know, I had never realised everyone else was in the same boat! For the first time in my life I was asked to speak without pretending. And I found I was not so different after all.

At last, approaching thirty years of age, I had found a source of values I could accept, having somehow not inherited the values of the culture I had been born into.

My eyes had been opened to this question of values at the age of eight by an apparently trivial incident concerning Vera, our housemaid, and very much a part of my life. I was living with my nanny in the nursery suite of the house in London, the home of my mother and stepfather, who had married a year or so previously. If Vera had come into the nurseries, to clean, to admire when I was dressed up for a party or to see the presents I had received for my birthday, she had not come as a visitor, as my mother had, but as an equal.

I had a crop of black-heads on my face, and my mother had been trying to persuade me to squeeze them out, or to let her do so. I could not see the purpose of this discomfort, or what harm they were doing left where they were. My mother had answered that everybody did, and that I would feel unpleasantly conspicuous if I walked around with this unsightly blemish. I thought of Vera. She had some great big black-heads on her face and had made no effort to remove them but nor, I was sure, had they made her uncomfortable. It had been on the tip of my tongue to say, 'But Vera doesn't' when all of a sudden the realisation had come: *everybody did not include Vera*. Within the unlimited world of people, I had discovered, there was a limited world of 'everybody'.

I went to boarding school when I was twelve; a small private school attended by some forty-five girls, all of whom came from the same strata of society. When I left school and started working in an office, for the first two years I lived with my grandmother. So it was not until I was nineteen that I left the world where 'everybody did not include Vera'.

And leave it I did. When the war ended and my grandmother's bachelor son came home from the Army, my mother tried to find some place to send me where nice girls lived. But the flow of people into London after the war made accommodation, already scarce owing to the combined effects of the bombing and the cessation of building, almost impossible to find. Consequently, it was not so much a case of selection but of finding anything at all. The house at Earls Court where I had my first taste of freedom had every discomfort, very mixed company, and was altogether not the sort of place my mother had envisaged.

From that point onwards, my horizons widened. It was not long before I was sharing a flat, and adjusting to visitors whose ways were very alien to my upbringing. My fellow patients at the sanatorium where I spent two years represented a good cross-section of society, so a further widening ensued. But it was when I was again established in London, in 1953, that I found myself in a society in which background counted for nothing, and here I felt I really belonged.

The Guest House in Swiss Cottage upon which my life centred for four years, did not have a name. It was invariably referred to as Number Five. From the outside it looked like so many in the district; a late Victorian family home. Mrs Brown, the American-born Indian Army widow who owned it, had not wasted an inch of space. Wherever possible rooms had been subdivided and filled with as many beds as they would hold — even the linen-cupboard had been turned into a little single room. What had originally been a house with six bedrooms and four maids' rooms now contained about fifty people, with more coming daily for meals. In spite of the cramped conditions, there was some sort of magnetism that held people here — maybe it was the contrast to most rooming houses, where one hardly spoke to one's next door neighbour. Mrs Brown arranged where everyone was to sit for meals and this gave her the opportunity to mix people in the way she wanted — she loved seeing the life that went on under her roof, and nothing delighted her more than to watch a budding romance.

Here were young and old, rich and poor, men and women. They came from Glasgow or Huddersfield or the West Country, from Australia or South Africa or Jamaica. They came from middle-class homes and from working-class homes — and I noticed with surprise that, by and large, it was the latter who had been brought up with the higher moral standards. The only thing we all had in common was the fact that we were willing to forgo a certain amount of physical comfort for the sake of the company we found here.

With the constant coming and going of people, the groups that formed were not so much cliques as nuclei towards which anyone might be attracted. Forgathering in someone's room of an evening or going to one of the local pubs, walking on Hampstead Heath or hiring a boat on Regent's Park Lake, I was in a society where I had found my place.

So circumstances had, step by step, led me away from the world where 'everybody doesn't include Vera' to one where people were just people, regardless of age, sex, colour, social background or anything else. It was now impossible to go back to thinking of myself as 'different' because of purely external circumstances.

If I had inherited my mother's values, they would have been based on just this notion of 'difference'. No doubt they were worthy enough, but the underlying, unspoken reason behind them, was convention dictating how a lady should behave. It had nothing whatsoever to do with the way, for instance, a shop girl might behave. The fact that 'everybody did not include Vera' did not mean that Vera, for my mother, had no existence, but that she existed, as it were, as a different species.

When I lived with my grandmother for the first two years of office life, she took very seriously the responsibility of caring for an eighteen-year-old girl, and tried hard to train me in 'right ways'. Perhaps her precepts were admirable, but I could not accept them. Her opinions had become encrusted within her and the reasons for them long forgotten.

My father, on the other hand, paid no heed to convention. His home in the North of Scotland had always been a place I delighted in, and in that area there was a common recognition that the 'difference' between those of high and low estate was one of circumstance and not fundamentally inherent. Skerrybrae, as his house was called, was a magnet for many people, coming in twos and threes, in tens or even hundreds, to accept my father's hospitality. On one occasion a naval captain was shown downstairs, having been newly appointed to the nearby Air Station. He had called here on his arrival because he had heard that my father was the uncrowned

King of Lossiemouth, and had joined the little group that was gathered round the cocktail bar, a veritable Aladdin's Cave of items collected from all corners of the earth. He was told to name his drink. However unusual the request, it would be produced.

However, my father was not a frivolous person. He took his duties as host very seriously, as he took everything he did seriously. He was interested in many aspects of local life, and when in a position of responsibility — for instance on the hospital's Board of Governors — discharged his duties with the utmost conscientiousness. His life was a ceaseless giving out of time, energy, patience and skill, and he was respected by everybody.

Surely here was a worthy source for values. But it was not so; there was something in me which yearned for *ordinariness*. His was a 'most' philosophy, but what I wanted to find was a 'golden mean'. So it was that I had not drawn upon my parental environment in the realm of values, and it was not until I came in contact with Coombe Springs that a valid source was presented to me, based not on *having*, nor yet on *doing*, but on *being*.

But surely, the reader may be thinking, the function of the Church is to act as custodian of values. *Being* and *doing* come within its province. So it should be. But though I might have been considered religious as a child — and I certainly attended church with enthusiasm — somehow I had failed to absorb the spiritual principles of Christianity in a coherent way.

When, at the age of eight, I had been told that we were to leave my grandparents' home, my first reaction had been to ask if we would still be able to go to church at St Mary Abbots. This has stayed in my mind because of the impression it made on my mother and the times I heard her recount the incident. I have often puzzled about this, and then one day, after I started to write down the events of my life preparatory to writing this book, the answer came to me in a flash. I had had to go to church at St Mary Abbots because *that was where God was*. I had not imagined God as a creature with arms and legs, or any other corporeal form, but in my mind He did have a location, and that location was up behind the altar in that one church in Kensington. I must at times have been in other churches, but they would have meant nothing. God was in this church, and as far as I was concerned He could not be anywhere else.

The God who resided in the church of St Mary Abbots was left behind when I went away to school. There did not seem to be any connection between Him and morning prayers, for which the whole school assembled, the five minute prayer interval in the evenings, or morning service on Sunday at the little parish church by the school. The two former were routine, and in church our attention was occupied with things other than the worship of God — particularly with watching the vicar so that later we could make fun of him and imitate him.

Our vicar had some quite outstanding qualities, but unfortunately they were somewhat eclipsed by the comic figure he presented to the world. He was over eighty years old, small, and looked more than anything like the figure that appeared on the front of the old Punch magazines; in the pulpit he was rather like a puppet bobbing up and down — he never seemed to bend from the waist. In his sermons he talked about the br-e-a-th of God — with deep inhaling and exhaling — and this was the motivating force of his life.

Nowadays such a man would not get through theological college — the dogmas and doctrines of the Church were something quite outside his scope; it was enough for him to serve God and love his fellow men. Here he was, over eighty years old, caring for a parish which included villages four or five miles apart, and no means of transport. We used to see him, summer and winter, striding about from one place to another, always happy. Once we met him when the ground was covered with snow and started throwing snowballs at him; he just laughed and threw some back — it was impossible to discountenance him or make him see anything but good in anybody. He lived all by himself in a little house which he kept spotlessly clean — two rooms and a kitchen and he went up a ladder to bed. Sometimes a group of us would be invited to tea, and spread out on the table there would be the most delicious array of home-made scones and cakes, all made with his own hands, which must have made serious inroads into his rations of fats and sugar.

When I was fifteen a confirmation class was arranged at the school, and I asked to be included amongst the candidates. I tried to persuade myself that this was not because everyone else was doing it, but I cannot think of any other motive. I did not conceive that I would be in any way different when I had been confirmed — I was making an act of affirmation, and did not look for a mystical content. But what was I affirming: Not a belief — I accepted the Christian story as I accepted everything; because those grown-ups to whom I looked said so. No idea of not believing had ever entered my head, so it could not be an affirmation of belief. Nor was it an affirmation that I was a Christian — I had no conception of what it meant to be a Christian, or even that there were any alternatives: a Christian or not a Christian. A Christian was what everybody was, I supposed — unless one happened to be a Jew. I would not have conceived of it, particularly, as a follower of Christ — in any case my idea of Christ had not progressed much beyond the 'Gentle Jesus meek and mild' I had learned when I had been taught to say my prayers in the nursery.

Then what had I been affirming? I would, I suppose, have said I was affirming the intention to lead a Christian life, which was to me the same as being good. And if pressed as to the meaning of 'being good', I would have said it was doing what I was told and not being a nuisance.

So the wheels were set in motion and the vicar came to the school once a week for the confirmation class. We were all very serious and did our best to bring him down to discuss such things as the Creed, but always, before we knew where we were, we were back on Mrs So-and-so's rheumatism or the Jones's new baby — he could only see his Christianity in terms of life. It was quite hopeless, and eventually one of the staff, who was a very staunch member of the Church, came to the rescue and took over the theological side of our instruction.

The day came. Of the service itself I can remember little — we had gone over it all so many times, of how we would kneel two by two for the bishop to lay his hands on our heads and say, 'Bless, O Lord, this Thy child . . .', and the occasion took its course. The valuable part of the preparation for confirmation had been the quiet times spent in prayer in the ancient parish church, when the first stirrings of religious fervour moved me. But although the experience remained with me, it did not occur to me that to go into a church and pray was not just something one did in the few weeks before one was confirmed; that instead of being an experience which had happened it could have been a jumping off point.

With confirmation, I had embarked on a life that was professedly Christian. Taking Communion every fortnight became an established routine, during holidays as well as term-time, along with taking myself to task the night before, and feeling afterwards that I started again with a 'clean slate'. That the Church was more than a building where services were conducted does not seem to have come to my notice. Consequently, when I had entered adult life and begun to look and see for myself what the world was like, religion had been thrown overboard.

All through my school days I had looked upon my parents as perfect. They could do no wrong and their words could not be questioned. And the same had gone for all the grown-up world. My Christian teaching had had the weight of my parents and all the grown-up world behind it, and therefore it must have been right, and I accepted it unquestioningly — and without thought.

Then, round about the age of eighteen, I had seriously considered my position and come to the conclusion that I did not believe. The Christian Story, the Virgin Birth, why did anyone believe it? They did not believe in anything else so illogical. My mother was a practical person, and if you had told her such a story and she had not heard it before she would most certainly have said, 'What a lot of nonsense'. A baby without an earthly father because God was its father; shepherds and kings following a star to find it in a stable; saving its life in response to a warning in a dream; the man Jesus, able to walk on the water, to produce enough food to feed five thousand people from two loaves and seven small fishes, to bring back to life a man who had been dead for three days; Jesus rising from the dead after he had been crucified; and going up a hill with His disciples and rising up into the clouds to be seen no more. If you had told her these things and she had not heard of them before, she would most certainly have dismissed them as nonsense. Anybody else I could think of would think it was all a lot of nonsense too. So why believe it just because the idea had been passed down, generation to generation, for two thousand years?

I had never come across any answers to this question. As a result, the whole Christian edifice collapsed when I reached adult life, and I was left believing in nothing. I supposed there was a God, some Prime Force behind it all, but I had no way of knowing about it or reason to suppose that it took any interest in me.

God was connected with church, and church was

connected with creeds. To stand up in what I still felt to be a sacred building and say 'I believe . . . ' unless one really did believe it was something I would never do, and I was very careful when I did find myself in a church, not to repeat any words whose import I could not subscribe to. This was perhaps a screen which prevented me from seeing that there was a value, a reality, at the back of it.

It was just because nothing was presumed, because the basis of his system was not blind acceptance but experiment, that Gurdjieff's ideas had first appealed to me. Then, through the agency of a man through whom I had learned much about my own nature — and of how little it differed from that of others — a new factor entered from the East, and I obeyed the simple injunction of our Indonesian mentors to 'give myself to God and let what happens happen'. With no alien idea or creed to act as a screen, the God-factor could now come into my life.

The work at Coombe Springs demanded everything one had to give it. Why did five hundred people put themselves through such hardship and inconvenience? If we had had to give a reason expressed in one phrase, it would have been that we were preparing for death.

Mr Bennett made this very plain in a public lecture he gave in 1954, which I attended as a first step towards renewing my connection with Coombe Springs after the 'false start' I had made the previous year. We all knew we must die one day, he said, but we pushed this knowledge to the back of our minds and lived as if it were not so. Yet when the moment of death came, if we had not acquired something permanent in ourselves which could survive, where should we be?

When I came back to Coombe Springs in 1954, I was quite certain that here was something vital, and on no account must I let go of it again. Mr Bennett, at his lecture, had been asked about this work being difficult. The question, he had said, was not whether it was difficult — of course it was difficult — but whether it was possible. He believed it was possible to learn to live rightly, and if it was possible then everything must be thrown into it. I had accepted that this would require a mammoth effort, and I put it before everything — in so far as the times set aside for going to Coombe Springs were kept sacred and no other engagement allowed to encroach, and I carried out the tasks we were set with a very fair degree of conscientiousness. It meant so much, and yet it did not mean very much — it was not at the root of my life, and yet I knew that if it meant anything at all that was where it belonged.

When I had first come amongst these people I had felt an impostor, for they had all seemed so single-minded. Still, to some extent, I felt an impostor. It was not until a further year after making this renewed contact that Coombe Springs became a place where I belonged.

Each summer we had the opportunity to stay at Coombe Springs for a week of intensive work. I had heard these seminars spoken of as being very hard, that one got up very early in the morning, and that great demands were made on the participants. Yet all were agreed that they would not miss them for anything. That year, 1955, with much misgiving I decided I would go.

It was hard, but I had reckoned without the impetus that comes under these conditions, that makes possible what would not otherwise be so. By the end of seven days I had learned for myself, from my own experience, what this work was. As we all sat, that last evening, round the fire which had been lit in the barbecue pit at the far end of the garden, eating the food which had been cooked upon it, we looked back at the experiences we had shared during this very full week, which had generated such a closeness between us. An entity, all of us, had come into being — an entity which I believe still exists, even though I have no idea what has become of most of those who were there.

We had made an impression, physically, on these seven acres, clearing ground of brambles and constructing a stream, and within the framework of the activities in the house and grounds the inner work had proceeded. Our lives had been ordered, vital, with energy which ordinarily goes to waste dammed and made to flow through channels which usually remain blocked.

This had been achieved by internal and external discipline. From 7.00 a.m. to 7.30 not a sound or a movement came from the eighty people in the dining room — that same room which two years later was to resound with the chanting of the Indonesians. To sit for thirty minutes cross-legged on the floor without moving and to keep one's mind so occupied with the *internal* task that no attention is left over to know about the increasing discomfort and pain which the body is trying to register, occupied all of us — and no one would have dreamed of arriving late.

By lunch-time stones had to be moved, floors polished, or flower beds weeded. And all the while we must be observing, experimenting, so that we could make a contribution to the after-lunch discussion. Five o'clock found us assembled for the practice of Gurdjieff's rhythmic movements, work even more concentrated and direct, as we struggled to synchronise the arms, the feet, the head into a harmonious whole in time with the music. And throughout the day we had to concentrate our minds on the subject on which we would be talking that evening.

Seven miles from the centre of London, we could have been in the middle of the Sahara Desert for all the impact the outside world had upon us. If the pressure was let down — which occasionally it was — this too was part of the pattern, and an opportunity for learning about oneself. For the rest of the time, we must not dissipate our new knowledge in idle chatter. When the day was over we went straight to bed, straight to sleep, and all too soon it was time to start again.

The pressure was let down that last evening as we sat in the summer twilight saying to each other the things that people usually say when they get together, but for which we had had no time before — Where do you live? What do you do? Do you have children? How old? It had been the last evening, but not the end — we would disperse at 4.00 p.m. the next day.

The next morning everything had changed. It had all seemed so important, so sacred, but now, as we tidied up and left everything in order for the next seminar, due to start the following Saturday, it did not matter, and I could not make myself care.

When lunch had been cleared away we sat on, for two hours instead of the usual half-hour, so that no one should go away with a question unanswered. I felt completely overwhelmed by the contrast between ordinary life and life as we had lived it during the past week. Today, the feeling I had had all week was not there, it would certainly not be there when we had all dispersed and gone back into life again, and I could not bear it. I cried and cried all through that meeting. We were living in a reality where outward appearances are not all that matters, and no one minded or was embarrassed. Towards the end I was able to speak about what I felt, to speak from the heart as I had never done before. As we left the dining room and gathered for the final cup of tea, I could see that many people were regarding me quite differently. I was one of them at last.

I had learned that it was possible to live differently because I had experienced it for a short time. So now I had a more concrete aim — to build up something inside myself by which this other state could be attained, not just in the artificial conditions of a retreat, but in everyday life.

'Do not work for results'. How often were we so admonished. This was a very necessary part of the discipline, for the immediate result of carrying out a certain exercise — the attainment of an unusual state, for instance — could be no criterion for judging its value. We were under a teacher, and obedience was necessary. We could use our own initiative, but if we went off on our own line, then we were heading for trouble. Often the exercises we performed yielded no tangible results, then suddenly something would 'click' and the result would be spectacular. Repeatedly someone, elated that 'results' had been obtained, would go off down that path, practising that one thing instead of keeping a balance, and it was obvious that they were stuck; they could make no progress.

Never could we be let off; never could there be an excuse for not working. 'There are times when you cannot do very much', we were told, 'but always there is something you can do.'

On another occasion we were sitting in our group meeting as we did every fortnight and, as was usual, person after person spoke of the small everyday difficulties they had encountered when carrying out the exercise we were engaged upon. Elizabeth, who was taking the group, would often cite from her own experience the way in which she had dealt with a similar situation, but however she answered, it was always in a practical, down-to-earth, matter-of-fact way, as befitted her nature. So, when she answered someone with the words, 'Yes, we forget that this is, literally, a matter of life and death', it came with all the more force. We did these exercises day after day, and needed to be reminded that our very existence — in its real sense — depended on our working in this way.

I was quite sure she was right — but only on a

theoretical level. As I carried out the tasks we were set, it was more like playing a game with myself than trying to rescue myself from extinction. To put aside twenty minutes at the beginning of each day to practise a relaxation exercise; to make up one's mind that one will be 'aware' at certain times of the day or in certain circumstances; to learn to perform an action using only parts essential to the performance; to learn to 'stand back' and 'look objectively' at what one is doing — the results we hoped to obtain if we continued regularly with such practices gave them a subjective significance.

The sum of it all we referred to simply as 'the Work'; those who came to Coombe Springs, and others similarly engaged, were 'in the Work'. The Work had an objective significance. Although we did not speak of God, we were treading this road, we believed, in order to fulfil that for which we were created. For Gurdjieff's was by no means an atheistic philosophy — on the contrary; in his major work, *All and Everything* (which was essential reading for us) frequent reference is made to the Deity in terms such as OUR COMMON FATHER OMNI-BEING ENDLESS-NESS. According to Gurdjieff, there was a universal Creator, but He was not interested in machines; if we could lift ourselves from the mechanical level, it would be possible to become instruments for His purpose.

To be connected with the Work was a privilege, a privilege that could only be given to a few since there were not the teachers to enable it to expand more than it had. The time would come when we would have the obligation to pass on what we had learned, but this would take many years. Reformers whose aim was to 'make the world a better place' were, we thought, presumptuous. How could they 'make' the world anything when they themselves were not anything? First they must act on themselves.

IV

'IT WAS VERY INTERESTING, all that he was saying, and there is just one question I have to ask', said Odette, the same Odette on whose bookshelf I had seen Ouspensky's *In Search of the Miraculous*. We were now sitting in a public house in London's West End, to which we had repaired after a lecture. It had nothing to do with Coombe Springs, but was another department of my life to which I was introducing Odette. It had been given by a man of whom I thought highly, and I was anxious to know her reactions. I looked at her enquiringly; what was the one question she had to ask?

'Where will you find the perfect people to live in this perfect world?' she queried.

No hypothetical 'perfect world' had, in fact, been put before us; but the lecturer had put forward certain principles and indicated that if society could be organised thus, more equable social conditions would result. Odette's reaction was typical of Coombe Springs, the inference being that the world is not right because the people are not right, and that once human nature becomes what it should be, then it will follow that we will order our affairs rightly.

It seems that those who are not satisfied with the world as it is fall into two camps — those who think it necessary to change human nature, and those who think it is the institutions which should change. I did not come within either of these categories for, it seemed to me, the two must be interdependent. Although conditions alone could never make a man what he should be, conditions that were not propitious could seriously mar his opportunities.

For it was not only in the personal field that questions had begun to arise when I grew up and looked out at the world. Parallel with the hows and whys concerning my life's purpose were the social hows and whys. During my childhood and right into my twenties I had accepted the world very much as I found it. That society was arranged, by and large, in the best possible way; that in every department of life those in authority had the knowledge and care to do what was best — these were things I had never questioned. As a small child I had often wanted to give money to the many beggars on the streets in those inter-war days, but I had never been allowed to and had been left with the impression that these men were not to be pitied but blamed, that the blind were not really blind but just pretending, and others were tricking the foolish out of their money. I grew up in a world where criticism was automatically directed towards anyone disturbing the status quo. No one had any sympathy with strikers or Communists or Conscientious Objectors, and it was not until I began to make contacts with people from a wider range of backgrounds that I had the first glimmerings of other points of view. Though when, in the election campaign which immediately followed the War, my grandmother switched off the radio every time there was a broadcast by one of 'those awful labour people', I did wonder how she could be so sure in her judgement if she never stopped to hear what they had to say.

The sanatorium at which I spent a good proportion of my period of illness was not in an easily accessible place, so visitors were few and eagerly looked forward to. It was most unusual, therefore, when I, who longed for nothing more than breaths from the outside world and had all the time there was for reading, found myself one day waiting for my visitors to go so that I could continue a book (*The Peckham Experiment* by Pearse & Crocker) that I had taken out of the sanatorium library. From this book I became aware of a group of people dissatisfied with the nation's approach to health - a subject about which I had come to have strong feelings.

By this time, having come under the care of some thirty doctors, seen the inside of three hospitals, two nursing homes and one sanatorium, as well as hearing of the experiences of other patients, I had lost many illusions about the medical profession. Although I had come across many whose only concern was to succour their fellow human beings, all too often I had observed that doctors and nurses, exploiting their patients' dependence on them, become corrupted by power.

It was not just the people, though, with whom I had become disillusioned: it was with medicine as a science. Below the surface of the great skill of the surgeons and the miracle-working drugs, lay a great abyss. I now knew of our ignorance of the human organism as a functioning whole. Too often had I seen patients ignoring all the advice of the doctors and getting on like a house on fire, while others who scrupulously did all that they were told made no progress. Leading as I was an abnormal life — in fact most of my life had been abnormal in one way or another — the sane, the healthy and the balanced had the most appeal for me. And here I found a super-normality in the story of the Pioneer Health Centre started before the war by some far-sighted biologists to study health in its positive aspect.

I discovered that one of my fellow patients also took a keen interest in this subject and had, in fact, given lectures on it. Together we marvelled at the changes in the lives of the 'guinea pigs' at the Peckham Health Centre. In the 'family consultations' the mutual understanding which had resulted had been almost as beneficial as the diagnosis and correction of disorders before they became chronic. In a clinical sense their health had benefitted, and it had benefitted also from the social opportunities they found. The organisers had aimed to 'cultivate' human life by providing suitable 'soil' — as a gardener cultivates plants by placing them in the right soil. Activities beneficial to the health of the members — using the word health in the broad sense of physical, mental and social health — would then, they had hoped, develop spontaneously. Develop they did; people who would never have dreamed of joining a club found themselves drawn into activities around them, and developing many hidden talents as a result.

It was not for the individual, though, that the Centre had catered; it was for the family. And it was the family that was enriched as each member went his own way, so that they were linked but not bound; it was the family that was enriched when a young couple could enjoy an evening among their kind knowing that the baby was sleeping soundly and safely in the night-nursery; it was the family that was enriched when a toddler could be gently weaned from its mother's skirt and she, by watching from a window overlooking the playroom could learn that she need have no anxiety about him when he was there without her.

But the greatest beneficiaries would be the next generation, for they would come in to families already functioning in health. 'Planned parenthood' included seeing that the health of the parents had been built up to tip-top condition before ever a child was conceived.

As my imagination had been fired hearing of a completely new conception of the problem of health care, so later, when I came back to live in London, it was fired on coming across a new way of looking at the economic life of the country. The health care vision had been put into practice on a small scale, serving both as a laboratory for experimental trials and as a model for national planners to look to. But the economic machinery of the nation applies to everybody and is itself affected by world conditions; it is not possible to isolate any group and make different conditions prevail. The organisation I now came in contact with could only work in the realm of theory.

The School of Economic Science had also been started by a small group of people who were dissatisfied with the orthodox outlook on an aspect of social organisation. The starting point of their ideas was a book written in the eighteen-seventies, Henry George's *Progress and Poverty*. Henry George had lived in America and had experienced the impact of the Industrial Revolution. At that time a book on the theory of political economy could still be a work of art; although logical and reasoned, it was fraught with the author's compassion for our human situation. Seeing the enormous changes taking place around him, George asks himself why it is that material advancements have not resulted in general human betterment. He states the problem in the first chapter:

> The present [nineteenth] century has been marked by a prodigious increase in wealth-producing power...
>
> At the beginning of this marvellous era it was natural to expect, and it was expected, that labour-saving inventions would lighten the toil and improve the condition of the labourer; that the enormous increase in the power of producing wealth would make real poverty a thing of the past. Could a man of the last [eighteenth] century... have seen, in a vision of the future, the steamship taking the place

of the sailing vessel, the railroad train of the wagon . . . could he have heard the throb of the engines that in obedience to human will, and for the satisfaction of human desire, exert a power greater than that of all men and all the beasts of burden of the earth combined . . . could he have seen steam hammers shaping mammoth shafts and mighty anchors, and delicate machinery making tiny watches . . . could he have conceived of the hundred thousand improvements which these only suggest, what would he have inferred as to the social condition of mankind?

It would not have seemed like an inference; further than the vision went, it would have seemed as though he saw; and his heart would have leaped and his nerves would have thrilled, as one who from a height beholds just ahead of the thirst-stricken caravan the living gleam of rustling woods and the glint of laughing waters. Plainly, in the sight of the imagination, he would have beheld these new forces elevating society from its very foundations, lifting the very poorest above the possibility of want, exempting the very lowest from anxiety for the material needs of life . . .

And out of these bounteous material conditions he would have seen arising, as necessary consequences, moral conditions realising the golden age of which mankind has always dreamed . . . For how could there be greed where all had enough? How could the vice, the crime, the ignorance, the brutality, that spring from poverty and the fear of poverty, exist where poverty had vanished? Who should crouch where all were freemen, who oppress where all were peers?'

But, he goes on to say, the world did not turn out like that:

Just as a community realises the conditions which all civilised communities are striving for . . . so does poverty take a darker aspect. Some get an infinitely better and easier living, but others find it hard to get a living at all. The 'tramp' comes with the locomotive, and alms houses and prisoners are as surely the marks of 'material progress' as are costly dwellings, rich warehouses, and magnificent churches . . .

The science of Political Economy, he says, should be able to provide a reason for this phenomenon. None of the current theories did, and from this point the book proceeded.

Henry George has become known as the Land Tax Man, for the main thesis of his book is the necessity for the abolition of private property in land. This he saw as the great injustice — that people should appropriate access to the fruits of the earth — and as the cause of the phenomenon outlined above: that the increased production resulting from the Industrial Revolution tended to benefit, not the whole of society, but a part of it. Henry George was not just a theorist with a bee in his bonnet; he was a philosopher, and one senses the author's growing awareness, as the book proceeds, that the natural order of things has a harmony and balance that it behoves people to understand and co-operate with. The current idea in force in his time was that poverty — and the degradation and misery that goes with it — was inevitable because improvement in living standards would immediately be swallowed up by an increase in population. This he disproves, together with other current theories. In his time, when men were dazzled by unprecedented material progress, he was very alone in seeing our civilisation not progressing but regressing.

He did not regard this recession as inevitable, however. 'The civilised world is trembling on the verge of a great movement', he writes towards the end of the book. 'Either it must be a leap upward, which will open the way to advances yet undreamed of, or it must be a plunge downward, which will carry us back towards barbarism.' He closes on a note of hope, of endless possibilities if we would but honour Liberty in form, not only in name. 'For liberty means justice, and justice is the natural law — the law of health and symmetry and strength, of fraternity and co-operation.' What might then come into being he describes as 'the Golden Age of which poets have sung', 'the culmination of Christianity', 'the City of God on earth', 'the reign of the Prince of Peace'.

The School of Economic Science was a dynamic organism; a 'school' in the classic sense, as in a school of painting. The students who enrolled for classes in the evenings, men and women of all ages and many occupations, were able to discuss the present state of affairs from first-hand knowledge. The tutors were not professionals, but students who had attended certain courses, had the necessary skill and wished to give their time in this way.

Henry George's book had been the starting point of the School and the eighty years which had elapsed since it was written had added weight to the author's contentions. But nothing was sacrosanct, and they were ever ready to move forward, discarding and adopting as fresh light washed upon the subject. And because the students and tutors were not withdrawn from the world but immersed in it, fresh light was continually being shed.

'But why doesn't somebody *tell* them?' asked a friend who had attended the School of Economic Science a little while and no longer had any illusions that the Ship of State was steered by competent helmsmen. The researches of the School of Economic Science reaffirmed the same thing as the Peckham Experiment — that those in charge treat *symptoms* and not *causes*; they do not understand the organism and its operation, but live from day to day and patch up as they go along.

Those who gave freely of their time and energy to the School of Economic Science, whether they carried out research or addressed envelopes, were responsible for the organisation or made coffee for the mid-evening interval, did so because they saw their contribution towards the betterment of their fellow men in service here. We were not an organisation which tried to do anything directly about what we saw around us. We believed education was necessary before that could happen — education, that is, in terms of fundamentals, as opposed to the so-called education of our schools and colleges. Ideas could permeate out and act as a leaven; then in time, maybe, change could come about.

It so happened that my connection with the School of Economic Science came to an end in the early part of 1955 — not many months after my renewed participation in the Coombe Springs activities. For the following two years my sole contribution to the general weal of humanity was to 'work on myself' in accordance with Gurdjieff's principles, under the direction of J. G. Bennett and his assistants at Coombe Springs. It may seem strange to the reader that I should even class it as such; it might seem that this 'work on oneself' was a wholly selfish activity. We at Coombe Springs did not see it like that: for us the leaven which the world needed was conscious people, and that was what we were trying to become.

So I ended the first thirty years of my life with a very different outlook to the one with which I had grown up. Far from seeing the world as a reasonable, ordered place, everything had conspired to show me how unreasonable, disordered and abnormal it was. My studies centring on Coombe Springs had shown me that the inner life of the individual is not normal; the data from the Peckham Experiment had shown that the life of the family, as an organism, is not normal; and from the School of Economic Science I had come to see how all the economic relationships — employer and employee, landlord and tenant, taxpayer and State, and so on — were out of joint. And in each case the result had been poverty — not material poverty but spiritual, a denial of the richness of life.

The life of an individual can only be described as poor when all that presses on her from outside is stronger than anything she has developed inside herself, and she is dominated by the opinions of others. How can the life of a family be described as other than poor when it has become shut in on itself, with no stimulus from the outside world, with physical or psychological disorders, not understood and allowed to become chronic, upsetting its inner balance and harmony? How can the life of a society be described as other than poor when at thirty a man's life has become fixed years before he knows what he is really fit for, and he faces an endless vista of work he can take no pride in, under conditions over which he has no control, the only outlet for his creative energies a small patch of back garden, and retirement at sixty-five the only thing to look forward to? And in all these cases I had seen that this poverty is not inevitable, that it is not right to deny ourselves the richness that life offers, and that the first step towards a life of balance and harmony lies in understanding.

V

HOW WAS IT THAT five hundred people practising a known and tried method of self-development, seeing themselves as an elite, and believing they were holding a sacred trust and fulfilling a cosmic role, came to adopt a practice so alien to their ways in its abandonment of conscious effort for submission to the Will of God? Mr Bennett's influence was certainly a potent factor in our change of course. We had put ourselves under his direction, and although he made it clear that this was an individual decision, the fact that he found it valid influenced all of us in its favour. That was not the whole truth. We had come here to fulfil our destiny of becoming conscious people; not to 'give ourselves to God'. Why did we not just carry on, ignoring this new byway which might divert us from our path?

The answer is simple and can be expressed in one phrase: *it couldn't be done*. Our endeavours made us see that life as it is lived in the world to-day is not the way that a human being — made in the image of God — was intended to live. We could get glimpses of this other, normal, life; we could even live it for a short period under special conditions — whenever we came back into the world at the end of the annual seminar at Coombe Springs and started to mix with the people outside, it felt like going into a lunatic asylum — but it was not possible to dwell on that plane. It was as though humanity were living at the bottom of a well, a well filled with dense fog. Sometimes we could rise sufficiently so that our heads came above the level of the fog into the clear air; we could even, on occasions, leap out, as a salmon leaps out of the water, but always we must return to the denser medium, to the fog.

Those of us who had only been engaged in these endeavours for a short time — and my three years was a very short time in this respect — still felt that we were getting somewhere; that we could fulfil our destiny in this way. But, although I did not realise it at the time, among the older hands there was a kind of desperation, a feeling that these methods had taken them as far as they could go, and still they were so far from being, in the true sense, human.

That Mr Bennett, while guiding and directing us over the years, had all the time recognised the inadequacy of his teaching, and known that something else would be necessary, came as a complete shock to me. When, in his explanatory talk after the arrival of the Indonesians, he made this plain, I felt almost cheated. Had he been leading us up the garden path all these years in letting us believe that what we were doing could lead us to wholeness and normality?

In the spring of 1957 I took my car to the Continent and, with two friends, had a fortnight's camping holiday. I spent the Sunday before I left at Coombe Springs — a day like so many others had been over the last three years, with no hint of something unusual about to happen.

The holiday was a physical and emotional strain and I came back exhausted. In the mail that awaited me on my return was a circular from Coombe Springs; Mr Bennett was to give some special talks on the significance of the coming to Coombe Springs of Pak Subuh, and it was important that everyone should attend at least one of them. The name meant nothing to me, and I wondered if it was someone who had been close to Gurdjieff. But in my present state of exhaustion I did not wonder very much. I looked at the dates of the meetings and saw that they had occurred while I had been away, heaved a sigh of relief that it was too late to do anything about it now, and dismissed it from my mind.

I was in the flat of one of the members of our group not long afterwards and discovered that she had been staying at Coombe Springs at the time. I gathered there had been a great upheaval during which she had been told to move out of her room as this was to be made ready for the visitors. Then better rooms were to be prepared instead. Everyone had been running round in circles. This did not sound like Coombe Springs at all; it was not usual to make any fuss of V.I.P.s — conditions were spartan, but those who came there came to Work, and did not expect anything else. Then the party of Indonesians had arrived and soon afterwards the mysterious New Work had begun. Within a week a temporary wooden structure had been erected in the grounds; somehow, in this crisis, men had appeared who could put it together, and more and more people were coming to Coombe Springs to take part. But what was it, this thing? What went on? What was it all about? That, my companion said, she would leave to Mr Bennett to explain. There were still a number of people who had not heard his explanatory talk which he was now repeating weekly.

I went down to Coombe Springs to hear the next one. I found about a dozen others, none of whom I knew, waiting to hear what he had to tell us. He spoke of Gurdjieff, and told us of an interview he had had with him shortly before his death in which he had said that his own work could only bring about a partial transformation in people. Another factor would be needed if humanity is to become what it ought to be, and someone else would bring this other factor — he was even then preparing himself, a long way away. Gurdjieff hinted that he should look towards the Malayan Archipelago and should read carefully the section of his book *All and Everything* about the legendary figure Ashiata Shiemash who had been sent from Above to the people of ancient Babylon to establish what Gurdjieff calls 'normal conditions of being-existence' by the awakening of Conscience within them. Mr Bennett had read and re-read the Ashiata Shiemash chapters, and he was convinced that they were prophetic; when Gurdjieff described events taking place a very long time ago, he said, he was often referring to the future.

Mr Bennett had long been convinced that the world

was about to enter a new Epoch. For years he had been speaking and writing about this, most notably in his book *The Crisis in Human Affairs*, published ten years previously. Since this conversation with Gurdjieff he had connected the New Epoch with the appearance of this man foreshadowed by Gurdjieff in his description of Ashiata Shiemash. He expected this great change quite soon — world events seemed to indicate it, particularly the return of the Jews to Palestine — but he had not thought it would occur during his lifetime. Three years ago, however, during a tour of the Middle East, extraordinary circumstances had led him to a man who had said things which he could have learned from no ordinary source. This man had then gone on to say that great events were to take place, he, Bennett, was to play a leading part in them; and that someone would come from the East and would even stay in his house.

Mr Bennett had come home bearing all this in mind. Shortly afterwards a letter arrived from a friend in Cyprus with news of a movement called Subud, originating in Java, whose ideas were remarkably similar to those of Gurdjieff and Ouspensky. Then Husein Rofé, an Englishman who had been closely connected with this movement and its founder, Pak Subuh, had come to London. Mr Bennett had learned from him that Pak Subuh could transmit a force which acted directly on the innermost part of a human being. Someone from the Malayan Archipelago? Ashiata Shiemash and the awakening of conscience? It had all seemed to fit. To receive this awakening, Pak Subuh's own presence was not necessary; Rofé himself was able to transmit it. Mr

Bennett had decided that he must try it out, and for the last six months he had been going regularly to London to take part in these 'exercises'. A few other people from Coombe Springs had also been going. Mr Bennett had become convinced that in this 'exercise' something truly remarkable took place, and that all of us should have the opportunity to receive it. An invitation had been sent to Pak Subuh to come to London and he had come. Now he was at Coombe Springs.

I had not gone that evening expecting to hear anything so drastic. I had to make sure that I had understood Mr Bennett's implications.

'Do you mean to say', I asked him, 'that the chief significance of Gurdjieff's life was to prepare us for this?'

'Yes, that is what I believe', he said.

If Mr Bennett believed that the chief significance of Gurdjieff's life was to prepare us for this, it must be important indeed. Little wonder that nearly everyone was willing to overlook the strangeness of the approach and to try it for themselves. For many, perhaps most, it was their subjective experiences during the 'Subud exercise' which convinced them to carry on. Those who did not have any such experiences themselves could nevertheless see that many did, and hoped that the time would come when their resistance would break down and they could 'experience' the exercise for themselves.

1957 was a fateful year in the history of Coombe Springs and for us all, and there could be no turning back.

VI

IN THE THIRTY-ONE YEARS which I had lived prior to this point, I had learned much from sources such as Coombe Springs, and I had also, of course, been taught lessons by Life itself.

Office life, which I entered at the age of nearly eighteen, gave me my first experience of mixing with people from a different social background. The work itself gave me something too. Most of the time I was adding up columns and columns of figures, or ticking off figures that someone else was calling out. But, although it was very repetitive, I was never bored by the work I did. From the beginning I applied myself to it and soon was able to do it quickly and accurately. Although I was an Articled Clerk — that is not simply an employee but an apprentice — in practice no distinction was made between us.

We did not work in our own office, but were sent out in groups of about four to carry out the audits of clients. Although the part of the audit done by the junior staff consists mainly of routine checking, the method must be chosen with some discretion. Every firm is different, and a short-cut where one system is in operation may be a complete waste of time with another. So I learned a lesson which has been very valuable throughout life — always to appraise a situation on its own merits. In our work, it was possible to look back and see how those who had carried out the audit the previous year had gone about it; but if we blindly copied what they had done, erroneous methods could be used year after year by people who did not think for themselves. So when a senior member of staff asked 'Why are you doing it that way?', 'Because that is how it was done last year' was never sufficient answer. 'That is how it is always done.' How often is that phrase given in justification of a course of action. Whenever I hear it a bell rings — unless it is the best way, then it is not justified.

There are two kinds of people, I always reckon — those who are basically happy unless something happens to make them unhappy and those who are basically unhappy but have their moments of happiness. I came into the latter category. It was only during holidays and other such special times that I could taste of life's sweetness.

These sweet interludes, then, were to be snatched at. I had no conception of the rhythm which makes ordinary, everyday things purposeful and even beautiful. I did not know that life is like the river whose current flows most strongly at the centre; that it is the byways that become stagnant. It was in the byways I had imagined Life could be lived fully. At the age of twenty, living in London, I thought with yearning of the night-clubs I had never frequented. I wished to remain single; not for ever — marriage seemed somehow inevitable — but at least until my late twenties. In the sanatorium, some of the women had thought that if you were not married, it was only normal and natural to have lovers. I lay in bed, day after day, determined to live a full life on my recovery, this 'full life' that I imagined certainly included lovers — there would be no restraints, I thought, when I made up for the years which had been lost. In short, the things which spelled Life to me then were in reality the living death of the stagnant waters.

The force which makes the stream flow is, in the case of the river, gravity. In the case of Life it is Love. There was, at that time, no love in my life; that was why I did not find that the middle-of-the-road is not dull and lifeless, but the place where the stream flows most strongly.

For twenty years, mine had been a life without love. A real relationship of love and respect had existed between myself and my grandfather in whose house I had lived from the age of five until my mother's remarriage three years later. During one of our last conversations he had said he was seventy-two and that that was quite long enough to live — he was not going to have a decrepit old age. I had been amazed, never having thought of him as old, but had accepted that if he said he had lived long enough, then that was so. He had been perfectly cheerful about it, and our relationship had been so much based on mutual respect that it had been quite natural that he should tell me, and that I should so readily accept his coming death. When I was later told he had died, I had felt no sadness.

Then, for twenty years, there had been no love. It was not that it had not been there. I had been surrounded by people to whom no amount of money or care had been too much to ensure my welfare. Whether because of my nature or because of circumstances I do not know, but I had somehow been impervious to love. I had had no love, and the fact that I might be loved had not occurred to me.

'Who do you love most in all the world?' I had asked my mother one day.

What had prompted the question I do not know, but I had been quite unprepared for the answer.

'You and Steve equally', she had said. (Steve was my step-father).

I had looked at her in amazed disbelief. 'You don't' had been my involuntary response.

'What do you mean, "you don't?" ' she had asked, very nettled.

Then, after a pause, she had asked, 'Well, who do you love most?'

I had known what I was expected to say, but I couldn't. I couldn't give an answer at all.

When my father had come home from the East, I, his eleven-year-old daughter, had been the only one left of his immediate family, and he would so have liked to have been proud of me. For years he had lived and worked in a place where the white man did not make his home, but simply amassed enough money to return to a life of comfort back in his home across the seas. This time had now come for him, and what a big disappointment I had turned out to be. When we had gone on shooting or fishing trips, either I would be afraid to get my feet wet, or afraid to get in the boat, or just not able to keep up.

Perhaps it was this sense of inadequacy that had helped to build up the barrier against love. For in all my environments I had felt inadequate. I had felt inadequate at the age of twelve when, coming back to London after my first term at boarding school, I could only admire from afar the new baby which had made her appearance in my absence, for she had been far too precious for me to be allowed to hold. I had felt inadequate in my father's house at Lossiemouth at the age of thirteen because the role assigned to me — that of lady of the house and hostess to all the people who came to stay, for meals, or for drinks — was one I did not feel equipped to play. I had felt inadequate at the age of fifteen when my mother, although she had 'flu, could not stay in bed because I could not be entrusted with the preparations for Christmas.

Whatever the reasons, I had entered adult life clad in an emotional suit of armour. 'You may be very clever but you have no feelings at all', my grandmother had said to me once when I was living with her in London. It seemed that my training to become a Chartered Accountant had led to my family deciding that in reality I was Very Clever, to compensate for the fact that I did not have much to talk about, or good manners, or a pleasing personality. However, I did have feelings, very strong feelings, but my instinct had been to protect what I had inside me, and so this 'suit of armour' had come into being.

Love had never broken through, though many would seem to have a claim on my love — my mother who would, I am sure, have made any sacrifice to ensure my physical well-being; my father who, having no wife, had looked to me to take the place of one; my grandmother whose favourite grandchild I had been. On my father's remarriage when I was twenty-one I had also had a stepmother who, having no children of her own, would have taken to her husband's only child. There had been all these as well as many others, but my 'suit of armour' had been too strong for them all. Glimmerings of what love meant had come through from time to time: moments of spontaneous wonder such as a sudden awareness of the beauty of nature, or a momentary recognition of another human being.

Such moments of spontaneous 'opening up' as a result of a shared experience or sometimes a solitary one had come to me from time to time, as they come to everyone, and these — the personal and the impersonal — I would put under the heading of love. There had been another sort of glimmering, too — a glimmering of the awareness of the Love of God. This had come in the ancient little church in our school grounds. The headmistress had told all confirmation candidates that we could absent ourselves from the lacrosse field and go into the church instead to pray. Most unhealthy for fifteen-year-old girls, the games mistress had thought it, but she had had to allow us our choice. The figure of

Christ on the Cross had become a focus for this glimmering, and it was an experience I had found very hard to explain away when, a few years later, I decided the whole thing was a myth. But although the experience had been so real, it had never occurred to me that it might be the beginning of something important in my life.

Twenty years of no love except for these momentary glimpses, no sooner recognised than gone. Then came one of the most elementary forms of love, which by the age of twenty-seven I had come to think had passed me by — that of 'falling-in-love'. When it did happen it was as though a dam, which had been slowly building up over the years, had been breached. With overwhelming force the flood waters hurtled through, and life could never be the same again.

Michael was my first love and my first — in fact my only — lover. The whole situation was fundamentally wrong, not just because it was against the rules, but because of this question of rhythm. I had no conception of the rhythm of life, I still had a 'snatching' mentality, and something which was basically good and true got out of gear. The relationship was wrong but it was not bad. There is all the difference in the world between something which is wrong and something which is bad. If it is bad it leaves a nasty taste in the mouth, one feels degraded and somehow coarsened as a result. This was nothing like that.

It all started when Mary, a fellow lodger at Number Five, left to return to Australia. We were sorry she was going, for she was a great magnetic centre and provider of cups of coffee. People had taken to gathering in her room and discussing such subjects as the meaning of life and whether there was a life after death, as well as more general subjects. One day I had been surprised to see what looked like a schoolgirl amongst us. It was Christine, who had come down from Newcastle the previous October as a student at London University. We became used to seeing her around, and by-and-by she permed her hair and did not look so much like a fifteen-year-old. Then the summer vacation had come, Christine had gone home and Michael, who had spent most of his free time with her, was now often to be found in Mary's room of an evening.

When Christine came back three months later she sat at our table for the evening meal. The top table had by this time become an institution — though people came and went, all fitted into a homogeneous whole. Christine did not fit in. She did not join in the general conversation, but whenever Michael's attention turned away from her she would find some way to bring it back, either by starting to talk of something exclusive to the two of them or, as a last resort, heaving a big sigh.

We did not see Michael up in Mary's room of an evening any more — his final examinations before qualifying as a veterinary surgeon were drawing near, and the time he could spare from his studies he spent with Christine. We would have been glad to welcome her amongst us for his sake, but he kept Christine and his friends separate. I was in Mary's room a few days before she left, along with Pam who shared her room.

'You don't think Michael is going to marry Christine, do you?' said Mary.

I looked at her, horrified. 'Oh, he *couldn't*', I said.

Although they spent so much time together, she seemed such a drain on him that I had not even entertained the idea. Mary, wiser in the ways of the world, thought it quite likely. We were all fond of Michael, though Mary and Pam knew him much better than I did, and we all felt depressed at this prospect. We thought Christine a little spineless, seeming to draw all her strength from Michael.

Mary said, 'Well, I'm older than he is, and before I go I shall tell him just what I think, and not to be such a fool'.

It was the eve of Mary's departure, and we decided we would go out for a drink. Michael came too, and about nine o'clock, seven of us went down to the pub on the corner.

A new drink, Merrydown cider, had recently come on to the market, and there was a conspiracy among the people who had sampled it not to warn anybody how strong it was. As we sat down, and Merrydown ciders were ordered all round, I had no idea what a bombshell this apparently mild and sweet-tasting drink was. It was only when we had all gathered in my bedsit for a coffee after the pub closed, that I found I was not capable of making coffee! For the first and last time in my life I was really drunk.

Number Five might seem to be just an ordinary guest

house in a 'bed-sitter' area of London, but for those who came within its orbit it remained the centre of their lives even when they moved elsewhere — it was the visible focus of a little community. Although by now I had a bed-sitting-room some seven minutes walk away, I still had my evening meal at Number Five. Michael had a similar arrangement. However it was not until a week after the night I had got so drunk that Michael and I were both at our places at the top table together. By this time Christine had left for the Christmas vacation. We stayed on talking after the other occupants had left the dining room, and then Michael asked me if I would come for coffee to the room he lived in a couple of streets away.

A week ago, with every vestige of social awareness swept away by the alcohol and too drunk to make the coffee, I had collapsed on to the divan into his arms. Michael and only Michael had existed for me. Perhaps my feelings and behaviour were due to the alcohol, but now, a week later and perfectly sober, it was just the same. He was not happy about his relationship with Christine, I was impatient with him, thinking he should simply write and tell her. Instead he drove over to see her during his Christmas holiday the next week.

I had no doubt that when Michael came back we would be lovers. I had already committed myself to this. No question of right or wrong in the matter entered my mind. I had worked out my own moral code. Men wanted sex and were dependent for it upon women; women, until recently, had been economically dependent upon men; marriage had been like a trade union whereby the women united to ensure that the men only got what they wanted on the women's terms; thus a woman who was 'immoral', a hundred or even fifty years ago, was execrated by the rest of her sex, in the same way as a workman who went outside his union and accepted lower wages would be execrated by his mates. That was the sole basis of 'morals', and it no longer applied in the modern world. The notion that I had missed out on a vital part of life loomed large in my thoughts, blotting out any other consideration. Experience was to teach me of its real significance.

I met Michael at the station when he returned to London. He was silent in the taxi, and obviously ill at ease. Later, sitting in front of my fire, he told me of his visit to Christine. 'As soon as I saw her face . . . She really does love me . . . I just couldn't . . .'

There was nothing else for him to do but go home. He put on his coat and we said goodnight.

This was January 1954, a little more than a year since Gurdjieff's ideas had first come to my notice. So I knew as a theory that for most of the time 'things happen' and we, who think we are masters of our fate, are really helplessly acted upon by forces outside our control. We do have power, but this power can only be exercised when there is a 'moment of choice'. These 'moments of choice' are rare and are often passed before they are recognised. Once passed, one just lives through the consequences, as a train which has passed a points junction must carry on along the rail.

One of these 'moments of choice' was now upon me, as Michael crossed the room and opened the door. I *could* have let him go out of that door, out of the house and down the street, without a word. It would have been possible. I had the strength. But I did not. Christine would not be back for another week. Then he was hers. But *this* week was ours, and every night we were together.

Then I had had my week, and it was over. I did not complain; I had made my bargain. If life had no more to offer, I would always have this to look back upon, to cherish.

I really thought it was like that — that it was possible to take one week and live it as if it was a self-contained unit. But life is a continuous stream; the effects of the way a week is lived — or an hour or a minute for that matter — are never-ending. I had made a bargain, I thought, but it was not a bargain that I had the power to make. How much thought did I give in the ensuing months to the course of action I should take — yet all the while I could experience my impotence, and was aware that whatever I decided events would take their course; there had been a time for decisions, but that time was past.

I had kept my bargain and not attempted to see Michael, but we were taking the same train into town each morning, Michael and Christine attended a party I gave (a great surprise, and the first time Christine had come amongst us socially), I had to move house and Michael helped with the moving ('I wish I was' had been his reply when I told him the taxi-driver thought he was my husband), he now passed my door on his way home, so he could look in for a little while — and somehow it became an established routine that every Friday night he spent with me. From Monday morning until early Friday evening he was studying for all he was worth for his final examinations. Friday evening until Saturday morning he spent with me, Saturday evening until Sunday afternoon he spent with Christine. And then the week would start again. It would have been a strain on a strong person — and Michael was not a strong person.

Although the more I learned of Christine and their life together, the more I felt how inadequate she was for Michael, at the same time I felt a great warmth towards her because we had a bond between us. Maybe she did love him, but her love was not as my love. Hers was exclusive, while mine spread out and, because I loved Michael, I loved the whole world. Although I wanted to be alone with him sometimes, I also needed to be with him in the company of others, knowing there was this thread between us. I had no need or wish for external attentions. When I was with him, the desire to give, to serve, was dominant, but not at the expense of my individuality; with him I was more myself.

I came to feel some of Michael's protectiveness towards Christine and she was no longer something to be brushed aside — the three of us, whether we liked it or not, had become a unit. Michael worried about Christine — her helplessness, her lack of friends, her different social background and the fact that his parents did not care for her — and she had become not his problem but our problem.

But the situation was not static. 'How I wish I knew what to do about that girl' changed into 'How I wish I knew what to do about you two girls.' The pendulum had swung and I knew that it was me he was wondering what to do about. Not so long ago he had come in one Friday evening, kissed me, looked at me despairingly and said, 'Oh, Angela, I can't give you my love, but neither can I leave you alone.' Now I knew he could quite easily leave me alone, and I should tell him not to come any more. But I put it off too long. I did not remonstrate, though, when he told me that that Friday would be the last time he would come.

It was less than three months since the eve of Mary's departure when we had all got so drunk, but in that short time what a metamorphosis had taken place — I was no longer the same person at all.

In none of the warnings I had had about sex had anyone ever told me the real danger — that when a grafting takes place the two cannot be separate without leaving a raw wound. Not that I accepted, all at once, that we would have to go our separate ways. My fortune had taken a turn for the worse, but it could also take a turn for the better in the future. I stayed around — and I suffered.

It was the end of the year before the final break came. Never had I thought it possible that I could not know what happened to Michael, but when he qualified as a veterinary surgeon, he left London and went out of my life. I had a job on the administrative staff of the college where Christine was a student. At the beginning of each term it was my job to give out the grants to the State Scholars, of which she was one. When she came into my office the following term and signed for hers, there was no shutting my eyes to the engagement ring on her finger. I remarked on it, and she said, surprised, 'Oh, didn't you know?' I smiled and congratulated her, and she went out with her money, leaving me weak and shaken.

The healing process was a painful one, but it was not a festering wound, so that in time — about a year all told — it did heal. In the meantime, the pain seemed to go beyond the bounds of endurance. A perfectly strange woman found me sitting on a public seat one day and said yes, she knew how women could suffer because of men. Another time my landlady came in to show a prospective tenant the room I was occupying. Having been alone, and not knowing what to do with the energy that welled up inside me, I had taken a pile of newspapers and was sitting in the middle of the floor, tearing the paper into shreds. The woman, who must have thought she had walked into a lunatic asylum, did not come to live with us, and my landlady was not pleased.

The worst incident was in Michael's house. I occasionally — perhaps once a month — took the initiative of going there to see him on some pretext. On this occasion I did not, as was usual, wait for him to come down from the top of the house to answer the bell because someone was going in as I got there. As I neared the top floor I heard voices coming from Michael's room, but I could not turn round and go down the stairs again because the woman was behind me. I turned and went into the lavatory to give her time to get into her room and shut the door, then after a minute or so emerged again on to the landing. A terrific scream rang through the house. With horror I realised that the scream came from me. In a matter of seconds I was down the stairs, along the street, and lying panting and exhausted on my bed, as though running away from something.

For all that the sequel was so painful, the experience had been a salutary one. I had been encased in a hard shell, but now the nut had been cracked, and it was possible for the light to flood in. I had learned a lot about life. I had learned that it is not something to be snatched at, but that it has a natural rhythm with which we must be in tune. I had also learned something of what men and women should mean to one another and of what a shared life could mean. Sex, I now knew, had its right and proper place in the context of that shared life, and to join together when the circumstances would not permit the joining was to court disaster. In short, what I had learned about life was its wholeness; that it does not consist of a series of experiences but has to be lived in its entirety.

Michael had made me aware of my incompleteness. Never, I thought, would I know with another man the complete absence of strangeness, the lack of excitement, the this-is-home feeling — in short, the fundamental *rightness* of coming together as if that was the way it had been in the beginning — as in the Platonic myth. I knew myself now as only half a thing, and the significance of marriage was the coming together to make a whole entity that could function as a unit. So much did I feel this that I could not look at the years ahead and imagine them without that fulfilment. Other men came into my life during the two-year interval between the healing of the wound that my liaison with Michael had left and the time when this book opens. I would probably have plunged into the first marriage that was offered, but it seemed to be my lot to be involved in complicated situations. At any rate — perhaps I was being protected again — the dangers which this attitude can lead to were averted.

PART TWO

'On this journey the traveller
abideth in every land
and dwelleth in every region'

From *The Seven Valleys*

VII

FROM THE TIME, two months before my eighteenth birthday, when I stepped out of the lift in an office block in the City of London, with the exception of the long break my illness caused, I had been an office worker. Two jobs in professional offices had been followed by positions on the administrative staffs of two London colleges. Then, in 1957, I moved to Coombe Springs to join the small band of helpers.

What a far cry this was from the ordered life of an office. The community at Coombe Springs had always had a fluid character, for it was recognised that for those who worked there, it was not just 'a job' but a way in which they could 'serve the Work'. The individual's contribution was his own responsibility, and except for the staggered day off each week, unlimited by 'hours of work'.

I had chosen to take up residence at Coombe Springs not long after it had been hit by the holocaust of the Subud influx. This is not to overdramatise, for into an environment already teeming with activity had come Pak Subuh with his wife, members of their family and other Indonesian 'helpers' — a party of about ten, all told. Moreover, at the time of their arrival the number of people living at Coombe Springs was already greater than usual, with rooms turned into dormitories to accommodate a number of young men engaged in the construction of the djamichunatra, and life was chaotic.

As news of their visit spread, more and more people converged on Coombe Springs — on the four 'exercise nights' of the week the house was thronged from six o'clock onwards, and it was often well after midnight before the turn of the last batch of thirty came. Those who were already resident at Coombe Springs felt that their home had been turned into a railway station.

The situation I came into three months after Pak Subuh and his party had arrived was verging on the chaotic. My main job was one which the rush of events had forced Mr Bennett's secretary to shelve, and for every hour that was left over from this, there was the demand of things to be done — the cleaning and other household tasks, which were left to anyone who could find the time to spare; the cook must have help in the kitchen; there was no one to be with Mrs Bennett — Mr Bennett's wife, who was an invalid and needed constant attention; there was someone to be fetched from the airport, or taken somewhere else. Those of us who were around to do all these things were very few and there was no one to co-ordinate our efforts; one just had to make up one's own mind which was the most urgent demand and turn a deaf ear to the rest.

One year later, Pak Subuh and all but two of his retinue have returned to Indonesia. The oriental trappings are no more, but the example of their gaiety and easiness, combined with the action of the force of Subud, has set us free, and no longer is there the intense seriousness of former days.

The transformation which had been set in motion by the arrival of our Eastern visitors is now complete. The phrase 'The Work' is no longer on anybody's lips; our activities, our aims and outlook — all are summed up in the word SUBUD. Subud was a *thing*, and we had settled down with it and were learning to live with it. The djamichunatra, or djami for short, was no longer a half-finished building surrounded by scaffolding. Though still not complete, it had now been in general use for some months, providing an appropriate place for holding the general sessions of the Subud exercise or *latihan*, the Indonesian word we now adopted.

This *latihan*, a practice of letting go and allowing this 'something' to take over, is the singular phenomenon of Subud. It was the cornerstone of our way of life. Its regular practice was taken for granted as a necessity for spiritual hygiene just as cleaning one's teeth is necessary for physical hygiene. We were now concerned with the Worship of God, and attempts to make something of ourselves by our efforts no longer had any place. 'This is the true way to worship God', Pak Subuh had said of the *latihan*. Its practice would lead to all good in this world and the next, and we felt our existence justified by the role we played in making it available to other people.

The house was no longer thronged with people four

nights a week — in the early months everyone had come to Coombe Springs for the *latihan* but now only those living in the vicinity came regularly, other arrangements having been made for those further away. Those who did come went straight to the djamichunatra, or to the coffee bar in one of the outbuildings. The rush of people had all been 'our own' people — those with previous connections here. As far as the world at large was concerned we had not existed, and Coombe Springs had still been a private place. It became a public place when the Eva Bartok story became known to the Press.

The 'miracle cure' of a film star by an unknown 'Eastern mystic' had brought the 'Mystery House' and the 'temple' in its grounds into full prominence in newspapers and magazines at home and abroad. Though the accounts had been so distorted, a small proportion of the many resulting enquiries were from people who had seen through the sensationalism and thought that here was a reality which might fulfil their inner need. The flow of people from the world at large had begun and was augmented as positive steps were taken to present Subud to the world as a method of spiritual regeneration. Now twenty or thirty 'outside' people were being admitted each week.

The *latihan* had replaced the methods of inner development advocated by Gurdjieff, but there had been no overt decision to cease our erstwhile activities. Every effort had been made to keep them going, but individuals had dropped out one by one. It was as though we had been pedalling forwards, but now were propelled by an engine. The time it took for the engine to get up enough steam so that the slower pedalling began to act as a brake varied from one individual to another, but as each reached this point the old activities had been dropped.

There was no longer any reticence in my own participation in the *latihan*. It had taken about three months to reach the point of freedom when my resistance ceased, and since then I had moved about freely and sung lustily. This power penetrated my body and permeated my daily activities. I could now appreciate that in Subud I had found something that was previously lacking. I was no longer merely playing a game. In Subud I had not only the aim of living according to the Will of God, I had been impregnated with it.

When Mr Bennett had introduced Subud to us, he had spoken of its objective, rather than its subjective, value, but with the hectic life and mastering the new approach, I had thought of Subud only in terms of its significance for us, five hundred people who came to Coombe Springs. It was some time before a conversation with one of the older residents caused me to look at it in a wider context.

'And to think that it should have come here', she said. 'It could have gone anywhere. We are no better or more deserving than anyone else, and yet it is here that it came.'

At once I was lifted out of my preoccupation with day-to-day problems, and for the first time looked at Subud on a world-scale instead of just a Coombe-scale; if there was little in my own experience to enable me to go all the way with my companion in her implication, neither did I reject it.

Mr Bennett had understood the global aspect from the beginning, and his approach verged on the apocalyptic. In the latter part of 1957 he wrote the book, *Concerning Subud*, to counteract the bad impression created by the Press. In this book Mr Bennett had written from the point of view of his own beliefs and experience. He had reiterated his conviction that a new Epoch was about to dawn, and that Divine Intervention would prevent humanity from hurtling along its present destructive path. He concluded that since mankind could easily be spiritually awakened, the beneficial results of a simultaneous awakening in many peoples in the world could scarcely be imagined. The implication throughout was that he believed Subud was what was going to save the world. Was that also what I believed? I could not be sure.

One of the press criticisms had said that Mr Bennett 'saw the hand of God in every favourable wind', and maybe we were all a bit like that. Events were moving so fast, and so much seemed to just fall into place, that we had no doubt that Providence was on our side. The building we now used for the *latihan*—the djamichunatra — was a case in point. Subud had come to Coombe Springs, necessitating a place for the *latihan*, and the djamichunatra was completed just as the local authority finally insisted that the temporary building we had erected without their permission must come down. Yet work on the djamichunatra had been started long before Mr Bennett had heard of Subud or known that it would come here. We did not think about it much, but as Subud grew and Coombe Springs became the focal point of a larger and larger network, we felt ourselves to be at the centre of the universe.

Shortly before their departure, Pak Subuh and his wife Ibu had appointed a number of men and women to augment the original small group of 'helpers' — those authorised to carry out certain spiritual functions — and, much to my surprise, I was among those selected. In this capacity, and later as Mr Bennett's secretary, I had much first hand experience of the workings of Subud.

It was the responsibility of the 'helpers' to interview enquirers; to 'open' new members; to 'take' the general sessions of the *latihan*; to attend *latihan* with those not joining in the general sessions; and generally to help anyone in difficulty or perplexity. 'To open new members' is a phrase that needs some explanation, for 'opening' or 'receiving the contact' gave Subud its identity. A number of people who had not 'received the contact', coming together for half-an-hour, closing their eyes, and giving free rein to the inner impulse would not have constituted the Subud *latihan*. Subud, as I have said before, is a *thing*. Pak Subuh had received it first, from him it had been transmitted to his wife, and so on. Thereafter, anyone who came passively into the presence of someone in whom it was operating strongly could also receive it. It was for this purpose that the 'helpers' were responsible for arranging 'openings'.

Whenever I acted as an 'opener', I was always amazed that, without any direct action on my part, *it* happened. It was emphasised that we must not in any way try to influence the people being 'opened', that they should not even be in our thoughts. After the 'opener' had explained that she and the other helpers were simply there as witnesses to their desire to worship the One True God, and asked them to close their eyes, to stand quite relaxed, and not to resist any impulse which might arise in them, we continued with the *latihan* in the ordinary way. Our worship of God and their worship of God were quite separate, but it was only human to peep occasionally to see how they were getting on. Usually every one of them had reacted physically and their bodily movements, often quite slight, demonstrated how the Power was working within them. Each time I was amazed. They could not understand, and on their behalf I felt an immense gratitude.

The 'throwing off' of impurities and their 'picking up' by others were features of the *latihan*, particularly at 'openings'. These 'healing' effects were not the result of an action by a person in the way that most non-material healing is. At one 'opening' there were just two 'openees' — a young married woman of about twenty-five, apparently in the best of health, and an older, rather decrepit woman. I was kneeling with my forehead touching the ground when I made to raise my head to see what the time was. There was a pain in my abdomen so intense that I could not move. Although the pain was in my body, it was not of it. I experienced it, but it did not belong to me. As the older of the two women seemed to have many ailments, I was not surprised by the experience. Neither was I disturbed at being quite unable to move — my whole attitude was one of submission, and I accepted that I would be kept in this position as long as it was necessary. Before long it lifted as though rising from me and up through the ceiling. Many months later, the younger of the two women happened to mention a disorder she had suffered from for years, which had caused her pain from time to time. Ever since her 'opening', she said, she had never experienced the pain again. 'So it was you', I thought, but I did not say anything.

The task of talking to women who came to enquire about Subud was a salutary one, for it was necessary to speak from one's own experience, and I found much value in having to take stock in order to express as sincerely as possible how I found Subud and what it meant to me. We had gone into it blindly, but they could now have the benefit of our experience. The message of Subud was quite simple. Thought, emotion and feeling are instruments by which we live our daily lives, and are not necessary for the worship of God. Subud acts not through these instruments, but directly on the innermost part of a person. I was amazed how nearly everybody understood and accepted this quite easily. We could not tell them how or why it happened, but that a very powerful mystery was at work there could be no doubt.

The nature of the Subud *latihan* made it necessary that it should be conducted separately for men and women. The men and women helpers, therefore, functioned independently of each other, and this applied also, to a large extent, to the administration. It had fallen to my lot to deal with the daily routine work on the women's side, keeping records, answering correspondence, making arrangements for new entrants, and seeing to anything else which cropped up. This work had been somewhat neglected when I took it over, and I found it satisfying getting things straightened out and in order, and took great delight in following the spread of Subud and its geographical distribution with the aid of a large map on the wall and coloured pins. With the ingrained idea that there is always a better way of doing anything, I got down with a will to devising a suitable system and operating it.

I felt myself to be in a position of some responsibility; in order to facilitate the work of the helpers, I aimed to have any information they might require available. I felt responsible in another way, too. For here we were at the beginning of something. My knowledge of human nature told me that whatever I did, the tendency would be for it to be slavishly copied in the future. But more than this, I felt we were playing a part in history and that in the future people would want to know as much as possible about the coming of Subud to the West. However, my job involved many frustrations. For one thing, we were very much in the dark as to what we were aiming at. As individuals we knew, but in a corporate sense we did not. Subud should be made available to those who asked for it, but in our responsibilities to those who came, in our relationships to one another, we were at sea.

Everyone who had been 'opened' was deemed a Subud member and our corporate name was The Subud Brotherhood. The phrase implied a relationship to be fostered, but whether we had a responsibility to play an active part in this fostering we did not know. It did not seem right that people should come twice a week, join in the *latihan*, and go away again, nobody knowing who they were or how they felt. Yet there were many whose only wish was to partake of the experience, who had come on the understanding that there was no commitment. On a practical basis, many questions arose, and there was no authority to whom to refer them.

I felt this lack of any structure very much. The release of pressure caused by the advent of Subud had resulted in a tendency amongst us to throw everything to the winds. This was compounded by the feeling at the back of many people's minds that it was a sign of spirituality to do things badly — one could be efficient or one could be spiritual. And it was fashionable to be spiritual.

My need of a structure, of some system of authority, was not shared by many people. But, involved as I was in the day-to-day workings of this thing, I saw the alternative. Problems cropped up and decisions had to be made. I had to have somewhere to refer questions of principle, and a group came into being to whom I did refer them. The group was neither appointed nor elected. Neither was I. We were merely filling a vacuum.

By and by, I became aware of more general problems. For example, Subud members living in an area might wish to hire a hall to meet for the *latihan*, this would affect neighbouring areas whose members would be drawn off; or maybe there would be insufficient helpers, raising the problem of whether it was necessary for visiting helpers to attend. It usually came out all right in the end, but I personally felt that, just because no system of authority existed to work all these things out, the result was a lack of co-ordination, as though a developing organism was all the time trying to burst out of a rigid encasement. From this experience, I came to a valuable conclusion about administration: if it is efficient, it is hardly noticed; if it is inefficient, it is all too obvious, and everyone grumbles that there is too much of it.

For the last nine months of this two-and-a-half year period of residence at Coombe Springs, I acted as Mr Bennett's secretary, and got some idea of the international picture. By this time Subud groups had started up all over the world, and most of them looked to Mr Bennett for guidance.

Perhaps it was rather a distorted picture I received, as so often only the troubles were written about — *A* could not get on with *B* and *B* said everything would be fine if only it wasn't for *C*. Often someone who had come to stay for a time at Coombe Springs started a group. Here they had seemed nice, pleasant people, but now we received nothing but complaints that they threw their weight about and made trouble. People were coming together who would normally have little in common, and difficult problems of adjustment resulted.

VIII

WHEN HE HAD LEFT US in 1958, Pak Subuh returned to Indonesia via America and Australia, where new Subud groups had started. After about a year at home, he again set out on a world tour whose highlight would be a Congress attended by Subud members from all over the world. The Congress was to be held at Coombe Springs.

A few days before it started, Pak Subuh arrived. All the residents were by the front door to greet him. How different the feeling now to the last time he was here — then he had been no more than an honoured guest; now he was coming into his own. He went into the house and, as always, it was quite impossible to tell what he was feeling. He looked round impassively, almost indifferently. Someone stepped forward and shook his hand, and the rest of us did not quite know what to do. He said a few words and then disappeared through the door marked PRIVATE, leaving a feeling of anticlimax.

The International Subud Congress of 1959 marked the end of the first phase of Subud in the West. A little over two years ago Pak Subuh had come bringing the *latihan* and we hadn't known what had hit us. Now he had seen its effect on Western people, we had had time to regain our equilibrium, and foundations could be laid for the future. Pak Subuh now gave us definite principles on which to work. A great deal of his advice sounded impractical, and I found it hard to visualise the end result, but at least it gave us all something to aim for.

Although I was unaware of it then, my sojourn at Coombe Springs was drawing to a close. Soon I was to go out into the world, and the Congress gave me something valuable to take away.

I had listened attentively to Pak Subuh throughout because the things he spoke of were the very problems we were constantly coming up against — about the *latihan* itself, about the functions of the helpers and other day-to-day matters — and what was not relevant to our own daily problems must be stored away because it concerned a question on which we, as helpers, might be asked for advice. But for me personally the most important thing which he said came, almost incidentally, quite near the end when he was answering some general questions.

The *latihan* was an act of worship, an act of surrender, but it was also an act of purification. Defects, bodily and psychic, were eliminated when we surrendered our wills to a wiser Power. As the function of the *latihan* was to purify, it followed that after it a person was in a state of relative purity. For some time it had been routine at

Coombe Springs for the helpers at an 'opening' to carry out a 'purifying exercise' or *latihan* among themselves first.

Pak Subuh had laid great emphasis during his talks on the importance of the nature of the sexual relationship because, he said, a child's whole life was affected by the state of the parents at the time of conception. Now he was asked whether, in view of this, a purifying exercise should be done before sexual intercourse, if conception was intended. He said it was very necessary, but not only when children were intended, and this did not only apply to sex for, said Pak Subuh, 'Every significant act is an act of worship'. One should also be pure for eating, for personal relationships, and for one's daily work.

Every significant act is an act of worship. This sentence burnt itself into my mind, and was the legacy I took with me when I left Coombe Springs for the larger world outside.

In writing of the impact on Coombe Springs of Subud and the Indonesians who brought it to us, I have used the word 'we', but this is misleading. There was not one way in which 'we' reacted, but many ways in which the individuals reacted. Some were extremely cynical, others completely uncritical, and there were many shades of opinion in between. On no aspect was there a greater divergence of opinion than in our attitude towards Pak Subuh himself.

I had thought little about the enigma of this man on his first visit, and it was not until we were watching someone's efforts with a cine camera and I saw Pak Subuh on the screen walking with Mr Bennett in the garden that the contrast struck me. Mr Bennett's movements looked jerky by comparison. Pak Subuh, always impassive, always perfectly relaxed, was certainly not of the ordinary run of humanity busying itself with trivia and banality.

Some people could not bear to be in the same room with him, and when a number of people gathered to hear him speak, almost invariably someone had to be taken out. There was no denying that there was a power about him, and the stories we heard from the men who were present when he came to the *latihan* were ample evidence of this.

During the Congress he explained his position, saying, 'Think of a school. You are the children in the classroom. Bapak is not the teacher — God is the teacher. Bapak is merely the janitor who arranges the chairs, the blackboard and chalk, and so on.' (Pak Subuh always referred to himself as Bapak, and amongst ourselves we referred to him in this way. It is an Indonesian word meaning father, and is commonly used to show respect.) Over and over again, he had denied that he was a teacher — he gave not teaching but explanation.

He aroused in me no feelings of any kind. He did not attract or repel. Passivity was his hallmark. He might say, as he did at the end of the Congress, 'It may be that you wish to be near Bapak and, on the other hand, Bapak wishes to be near you, his children', but that was not how it seemed to me. If anything, one could detect a slight distaste in the way he regarded us. He was here because he believed it was the Will of God, but I had the feeling that he did not really belong amongst us — almost as though he had strayed on to this planet by mistake.

Many people sought personal interviews with Pak Subuh and asked him what they should do with their lives. He left Coombe Springs soon after the end of the Congress to continue his world tour, and it was at his last stop in the British Isles — Edinburgh — that I eventually came face to face with him with only an interpreter present.

The interpreter explained that I was Mr Bennett's secretary. I asked if what I was doing was right for me, for Mr Bennett, and for Subud. I knew that whatever he said, I would do. It was pointless asking, and then only doing it if the answer was agreeable. I had chosen to lay my affairs in his hands.

Without any hesitation, he said, 'This is where you should be; here in Edinburgh.'

He seemed almost surprised himself that he should have been so emphatic, and appeared to be feeling round for confirmation. Slowly he said, 'Coombe Springs — no; London — no; Glasgow — no. No, it must be Edinburgh.'

Other people who had had interviews with Pak Subuh had been told that the right place for them to be was somewhere on the other side of the world. Edinburgh, by contrast, seemed undramatic, to say the least. Then came the realisation that Edinburgh was indeed where I should be. I felt that I had been shown what I had known all the time.

Two years earlier my father had had a house built on

the outskirts of Edinburgh and he and my step-mother had moved there from Lossiemouth. In the past, when I had been in Lossiemouth on holiday they had discouraged me from returning to my Guest House life and office job in London, saying it would be much better for me — and particularly for my health — to remain there with them. Although there had been little to attract me to London at the time, I had felt that I had to return, that London was the place for my life to go forward. Edinburgh was a different situation; I could live my own life in the city and they would be nearby.

I asked Pak Subuh what I should do here. He had no feelings about this. He asked me what I was trained for and said, laconically, that yes, office work was all right for me.

So it was that, after two-and-a-quarter years, my sojourn at Coombe Springs ended. I now had a vastly different conception of my role in the scheme of things from that which I had had before encountering Subud. In the past we had seen ourselves as members of a small elite. I had once been told by a woman who had been coming to Coombe Springs for many years, and who now had a school-age family, that when she had had her babies this had been frowned upon — there were plenty of people in the world who could have babies. The few who had been entrusted with The Work had been called to higher things.

Subud had thrown the doors of Coombe Springs open to people from many backgrounds — I do not mean social backgrounds, for these had always varied, but spiritual backgrounds. People did not come to Subud from nothing; nearly everyone had been following some method or way. And listening to so many diverse attitudes and opinions we had become much more humble. Subud had set us free in another important way too; it had freed us from our complete dependence on Mr Bennett.

'What would we do if anything happened to Mr B?' I remember someone asking me once. He would not live for ever; we would have to do without him. We had thought it unimaginable, but gradually looking outside ourselves for guidance had become foreign to us and we became less dependent on him.

Coming from a Christian culture it was natural for us to compare the inexplicable things of Subud with the Christian story, to read the Acts of the Apostles and wonder if this force we had experienced was the same Force evident at Pentecost?

Whether it was or not, Pentecost, along with other inexplicable happenings in the New Testament, I no longer found invalid because there was no material cause for them. It had become a commonplace experience for things to happen without a material cause. Another effect of Subud had been to cause me to look outwards to the churches. From the beginning Pak Subuh had emphasised that Subud was not a religion, and had advised us to continue to follow the practices of our religion as well as coming to the *latihan*. As with most of us here, however, I did not have a religion to follow. After a time I had begun to wonder whether I should have, whether the inner reality of the worship of God should have a channel.

For the first year of my stay at Coombe Springs, all my interest and activity had been bound up in what was taking place there, but afterwards my life became less monastic, and I began to look outwards. In the past I had never questioned why I went exclusively to the Church of England, but now I decided to take a look at the various denominations, Sunday by Sunday visiting most of the Nonconformist churches in the nearby town of Kingston-upon-Thames. Eventually, after nearly fifteen years, it felt right for me to take Communion.

Subud people tended to look down on the churches, believing they were all form and no substance. One evening, however, not long before I left Coombe Springs, I was struck by a real contrast. A group attached to the Kingston Baptist Church — my favourite — regularly socialised after the evening Service, and I was invited to attend. I went straight from this meeting to a party full of people from Coombe Springs including one girl, sinuously posturing, with knotted shirt and bare midriff.

A few people coming together, talking, drinking. I could not put my finger on anything about the gathering that was wrong. Yet everything was wrong. It was like entering a stuffy room. I was forced to the conclusion that although Subud may have something the Churches had not, they also had something lacking in Subud.

By the time I left Coombe Springs, I had gained in humility and openness, aware that much more was at work in the world than happenings in my own little corner.

I did not believe in the uniqueness of Subud. Pak Subuh had said many times that God had sent this thing into the world at this particular time in response to a particular need. In times past, he said, God had guided mankind by way of the Prophets — Abraham, Moses, Jesus, Muhammad — but Muhammad, the Seal of the Prophets, had been the last. The channel for God's Grace now, he implied, was Subud. There were people, however — not many, but more than one or two — who when they were 'opened' said that the experience was not new to them. It was usually supposed that they had imagined it; only through Subud could this happen. Personally, I heard it said too often and too definitely not to believe it.

So I did not believe that Subud was unique. It was my way of seeking to do the Will of God, and that was enough. Pak Subuh I believed to be the first person to receive the gift of Subud and to be aware of things of which we were unaware but, like anyone else, he had his limitations.

However, in all the lessons of my thirty-three years to the time I came to leave Coombe Springs, I had learned very little about love, that is, about love as a conscious and responsible emotion. I remember a mother of two children at Coombe Springs once telling me how difficult she found it to share her love equally between them. It was the first time I had heard of the notion of a responsibility to love. My next lesson in a new life and a new place was to be a lesson in this responsibility to love not just our families or those near to us, but on a much wider scale.

IX

THE DAY CAME when I was to leave Coombe Springs. I packed everything I possessed into my car and set off. During the past two and a quarter years I had had many responsibilities and little leisure. Now I had lots of leisure and no responsibilities. For once, I was not bound by time. I realised how little I knew this country I lived in, and decided to make my way north, like a tortoise with his house on his back. The first port of call was a hut in the New Forest: Kitty's Hut.

Since she started Subud in September 1958, Kitty had spent most of her time at Coombe Springs, only returning occasionally to her own domain. Subud had been like a bombshell in her life. Most of us had had no idea what a searing experience it all was for her — we had thought her rather flamboyant, full of big ideas, but not very reliable. Nobody had taken her expressions of deep feeling and occasional outbreaks of poetry seriously. I had got to know her better as time went on, but it was not until I met her on her home ground, as a guest at 'The

Hut' one summer's weekend in 1959, that I began to see her as she really was; wholly responsible and fully in tune with her environment.

And what an environment! I had not known what to expect when I had gone down there, for I knew 'hut' was not merely a whimsical name, but a fairly accurate description of what it actually was. It was actually two huts — you entered through the smaller one, which served as a kitchen, and a short passage connected it with the larger, bed-sitting room. Kitty did not live *in* the Hut as one would live *in* a house; her home had no perimeter — it was not bounded by anything. She lived on the moor — the term New Forest is misleading, as in that part of it there is hardly a tree to be seen. There were the walls and roof to protect her and her possessions from the weather, but they did not enclose. The world of switches and taps and lavatories had been left behind. She used no chemicals; following a few simple rules of hygiene, they were unnecessary and what came from the earth was returned to it.

Kitty always got up very early, and the morning of my stay had been so glorious that I also got up at six, and after a cup of tea was away up the hillside and over the moors. It had been scorchingly hot weather — much too hot to do any walking during the day, but at this hour, when everything was fresh and covered with spiders' webs revealed by the dew, it was perfect. For two or three hours I had roamed up there, returning just as Kitty decided it was breakfast time. During the day it was too hot to do anything but lie in the shade, and I read parts of the book Kitty was writing — amazed that she had such a variety of experience in her life. At night the stars were so clear. I stayed a second night, and caught the early train on the Monday morning, thoroughly refreshed by my stay.

'So now you know that the Hut is always here as a place of refuge', she said. 'If your lover had deserted you, your children been drowned, and your life's work lay in ruins, still you would find peace here.'

I had been enchanted with the Hut in that sizzling July weather. It was also marvellous in the winter, according to Kitty, but I had not been able to imagine it. Now it was winter and, with only the hurricane lamp left burning to mark the point on the moor to stop the car, I made my way through the gate and along the path, picking up the lamp as I went, and came into the Hut from the dark winter's night to a warm welcome and a roaring fire. I saw immediately what she meant. The large brick fireplace was made up with a good fire of coal and wood, a large black kettle was simmering on the hob, a heavy velvet curtain was drawn across the door — and the oil lamps cast their soft light. I was still conscious of being on the moor as the wind whistled round and the rain battered on the windows, but it was a warm and cosy haven inside.

It was ten o'clock, and I had said I would be there about six, but 'we felt that you were all right', said Kitty — she had a neighbour with her — 'that you were on your way and had come to no harm.'

The following afternoon Kitty suggested that since I

had no definite plans, I might like to stay on to do some typing for her and live in a nearby caravan. We went down to look at it; it was small but I tried the bed and found it just long enough for my six-foot frame. I agreed. Kitty was going to London the next morning and would not be back until the evening of the following day. By that time I would be able to have the caravan well aired and have moved in. As I said I would like to start on the work right away and not wait until she returned, she spent some time sorting through her papers before she left in the early morning.

The proposition to stay in the caravan had been made in broad daylight. I had not visualised how it would be, going down there in the dark. I could not bring myself to walk down the path, away from habitation, through the bushes and the bracken. I would have died of fright.

Even in the Hut I became fearful as darkness closed in. It became impossible for me to go into the kitchen; I had to stay where I was. Even in the cosy living area, fear crept closer around me. The oil lamp had worked all right the previous evening, but now it flickered and went out, and I did not know what to do. I lit all the candles I could find. I took a book from the shelf and lay in front of the fire and read. The blankets on the clothes horse made a screen behind me, so that even when all the candles but one had gone out, inside this little square with the fire on one side and screened by the blankets on the other three sides, I felt I was all right. The fire was getting low and I had not had the forethought to fetch more coal and wood before it had got dark. The light from the one candle was enough to read by, so I lay there, almost too petrified to move. Smells came wafting from the kitchen where I had put a casserole in the oven, but I would rather have faced wild beasts than gone in there to see how it was getting on. Inside this little circle I was safe — so long, that is, as the candle lasted. That gone, and the outer darkness would converge upon me, and I would be destroyed. I looked at the candle getting shorter and shorter, and that was all my consciousness could encompass. The only question in the world was whether Kitty would come in time.

Why, in this extremity, did I not turn to the power of the *latihan*. Surely this was a time to use my awareness of the presence of God. But I was on the very brink of the amount of fear I could stand. The *latihan* is itself a step into the darkness and often brings its own fears. I was not willing to take the risk. No, I would stay as I was, because this I knew I could bear and no more.

Kitty did come before the candle was finished and, as I had known, her presence made all these fears seem ridiculous and unreasonable.

When Kitty was feeling anything, the feeling pervaded her, filling all of her large frame, and even then she could not contain it. I was not left in ignorance of what she was feeling when she came in and found things as they were. She had to grope her way in because it was so dark. The fire was low. The Hut was no place to come home to. The blankets were draped around and my things were lying about. I had burnt the wick of the lamp down by trying to light it when it had run out of oil, and I had used all the candles. To make matters worse, I had forgotten we were expecting a visitor and that this would be a Subud evening. She did not direct abuse against me, she just welled up with emotion, and exploded, and explained, quietly enough, just how it had struck her when she had come in. She did not ridicule my fear, fear was real, that she recognised. But it can also be overcome.

It was obvious I was not going to spend the night in the caravan — all the bedding and all my things were still up here, and anyway I would be much too scared. Kitty pointed out that she had never said I could stay another night in the Hut — the arrangement had been that I would have moved out and into the caravan by the time she got back. 'I don't know', she said. 'I always think that people are going to do what they say.' And here was I — I had arrived about four hours later than I had said I would, I had not moved down to the caravan, I had offered to start the typing while she was away, she had therefore prepared it before she left in the morning and I had not done any. What possible grounds had I for taking it for granted that I could just stay in the Hut?

It was not in my nature to beg or plead, and anyway, I had not a leg to stand on. So I started to get dressed and put my things together. There was nowhere I could go at that time of night. The only home I had was my car; I would go there and if it was too late to stop anywhere, I would just drive on through the night.

Kitty sat and considered and then said quietly, 'No. That would not be right.'

The next morning we considered the situation. The caravan was out but I could still have it to type in the day. I decided that I would stay, and managed to find a room in the village where I could sleep.

I knew what I was in for. 'I shall continue to bash you about', said Kitty, for her emotional force could reduce me to pulp. It was something I had not experienced before — I might call it positive anger.

I had often been faced with negative anger, usually in the form of a torrent of abuse, and always stemming somehow from guilt, which left me weak and uncomprehending. Kitty's was just the opposite to this, for it was not rooted in guilt, but in love. She could speak quite quietly, but with tremendous force, and because it was rooted in love, it had positive results. It held a mirror up to me that allowed me to see how I was, and I submitted willingly to her constructive criticism.

Although much that I had learned at Coombe Springs stemmed from order, I had never found it worthwhile to put the personal things around me in order. Kitty, on the other hand, had a positive belief in the value of Order. In these primitive surroundings it was a necessity; there was only just room in the Hut for everything if it was in its proper place. Timing, too, became important because some things had to be done before dark.

Others had tried to shake me from my disorderly ways before, but without effect. Kitty, however, did have an effect. 'Nothing has any significance', she once said, 'except what is done from the motive of love.' And that was her motive in trying to instil some kind of order into me, so it worked. In a flash I saw that this is quite literally true. One can spend time, energy, care, thought and goodness knows what on something, but if the motive of love is not behind it all, then no amount of these things can be of any avail, no result can be obtained and one might as well have saved one's breath.

I learned many lessons during this time with Kitty, and the greatest was this lesson of love. For she had an innate sense of her oneness with all humanity, and so she respected you. She had true humility; she could criticise, but never as someone who knew talking down to someone who did not. Despite her greater understanding, experience and years, there was an equality between us. The desire for rightness was her motivating force, but she did not deny herself the pleasures of life — far from it. I found her very salutary because self-denial for its own sake was something very much ingrained in me — as though it was wrong to have for myself anything of quality because I was not worth anything.

Perhaps the most valuable thing that Kitty did for me was to love me for myself. Her whole attitude said, in effect, 'You matter'. I mattered to her because I was a child of God. I mattered to her, and I must matter to myself, because if I thought I did not matter I was saying that one of God's creatures did not matter. Consequently, whatever I did, thought, said, all mattered. If I went out in the morning without making my bed, it mattered. Kitty lived very much in a physical realm; *things* were important to her: sizes and shapes and colours, reflecting many years' study of Rudolph Steiner's ideas and methods. This philosophy of mattering extended to the things she used and the things around her; it mattered whether you were surrounded by ugly or beautiful things, for example.

We often talked about prayer, a subject I had hitherto given but scant attention. I do not remember it ever cropping up in the group meetings of our pre-Subud work at Coombe Springs, though I do remember Mr Bennett, at a seminar, stressing the need to pray for the dead. In the *latihan* one turned towards God in complete passivity and submission to His Will, and to go further and reach out, ask for anything, had seemed inappropriate. It had surprised me when I had heard that Ibu, Pak Subuh's wife, had advised someone in a particular situation to pray. It had turned out that in her case the disturbance of the *latihan* had been deemed inadvisable. Prayer did not disturb as the *latihan* disturbed. I had put this information at the back of my mind in case it should ever be needed. It had not occurred to me that prayer in general was a thing one had need of even if one had the *latihan*.

Kitty approached it from another angle. 'It works', she said, and in such a way that I believed her. She once worked for the London Healing Mission, an organisation which received requests from, or on behalf of, the sick, and sent their particulars to members all over the country, who would then pray for these people. The results had left her in no doubt of the effectiveness of what had been done. She often, too, gave examples from her personal life when she had asked for something and her prayer had been answered.

So that was a good starting point: it worked. But there was more to it than that. I had touched on something very big, and it was most important I should understand more about it. Kitty talked about God with great familiarity; He was an ever-present reality to her. Many people think they believe that God can do anything, but Kitty had complete confidence in this, and gradually it began to sink in that this was the most powerful thing. Then an incident occurred which proved it had not sunk in very far. Some difficulty cropped up — I cannot remember what it was.

'What can we do?' I asked.

'We can pray', said Kitty.

'Oh, yes', I said, impatiently, 'but I want to do something practical.' Kitty gave me a look that threw my words back in my face and made me realise the import of what I had said.

Quietly she responded, 'I can't think of anything more practical.'

Kitty was a Christian, not in the usual sense, but a person in whose life Christ played a special role, a role I could not understand. Her awareness of God was innate; even as a child she had been sure of it, though her parents had been atheists. But her Christianity was something extra to this, something that had come to her in adult life, and was very important. I very much wanted to understand the part Christ played in her scheme of things. He had something to do with order and the formative forces. Once she said that if I found myself surrounded by chaos — chaos of my own making — I could make the sign of the Cross on my forehead. I never did bring myself to do it. Perhaps I felt I must have more understanding before using such a powerful symbol. But though not understanding it, I was always aware that in the Hut I was in a Christian environment.

Since reading Alice Bailey's autobiography a year or two previously, I had intended to get hold of some more of her works, but it was not until I had come to the Hut that I had done so. Her *Reappearance of the Christ* was the book I had picked up and started to read on that evening when I had been so frightened, and I continued with it later. The ideas were not new to me, but seemed fantastical. She wrote with such self-assurance of the Christ waiting to reappear from the Himalayas and establish the New World Religion, of the Hierarchy who would be His Disciples, of a body called the New Group of World Servers, and so on. None of this struck any chord of reality, and she gave no clue as to why she should have this information, its origin or her authority to divulge it. However, the force and urgency of the way it was written captured my imagination. She seemed to gather up the expectancy felt in all parts of the world, within and without the various organisations, religious and secular, that something would happen soon to put the world aright. For the last two thousand years, she wrote, we had been living in the Piscean age. Now we were moving into the Aquarian age, when the Christ would come and finish the work He had started two thousand years ago.

An awareness that a New Age had dawned pervaded Kitty and the Hut. Everything she did was related to this knowledge. Her Christianity was not denominational — she attended the parish church, Quaker meetings and had until recently preached regularly in Congregational churches — but to her the Christian Community, the sect founded on Rudolph Steiner's principles, represented Christianity for the New Age. The New Age gave life meaning. Everything took on a new significance.

Pinned up on a wall of the Hut was a copy of Alice Bailey's invocation. Kitty attached a great deal of importance to this, and used it regularly. Sometimes instead of Grace before a meal one of us would read it:

From the point of Light within the Mind of God
Let Light stream forth into the minds of men
Let Light descend on Earth.

From the Point of Love within the Heart of God
Let love stream forth into the hearts of men
May Christ return to Earth.

From the centre where the will of God is known
Let purpose guide the little wills of men —
The purpose which the Master knows and serves.

From the centre which we call the race of men
Let the plan of Love and Light work out
And may it seal the door where evil dwells.

Let Light and Love and Power restore the Plan on Earth.

The New Age had dawned and soon — perhaps even within my lifetime — we would see the establishment of the Kingdom of Heaven on Earth. The idea was not new to me but it had come to the fore during this period with Kitty. She was permeated with it and I became infected.

But one day, when Kitty and I had gone out for a walk together, she said something for which I was not prepared, and if she had not said it with such force, I would have dismissed it as ridiculous. Talking about the Kingdom, which Alice Bailey and others said was to come, she said, 'This is not something in the future. It is here, now.'

She could not mean that.

'Next time you go to London', I said, 'just stand and watch the people going by. Look at their faces. How can you say that this is the Kingdom of Heaven on earth?'

'I know; you are quite right,' she said. 'But I know I am right too.'

With Kitty, everything had significance, and she imparted her joy in everything around. Kahlil Gibran's *The Prophet* had recently become a favourite book of mine, and I thought of its words: 'The deeper that sorrow carves into your being, the more joy you can contain.' Kitty was a good example. I knew her life had contained great difficulties.

I do not know why I wanted to leave Kitty's. I had learned much, but I felt she held the key to learning much more. I think I felt like someone who has had good food and knows that it must be digested before any more can be assimilated. The important thing was that she had initiated new trends of thought, which were to stand me in good stead. Moreover, all that had taken place in these weeks had nurtured feelings of love in me. If Kitty had been less mature and less wise, this love might have flowed down the wrong channels. I am grateful this was not allowed to happen.

Nothing has any significance except that which is done from the motive of love. Many people would agree with that sentiment — or think they would. Few really do. But the more you live with it, the more you realise it is true, and you stop thinking you can achieve anything any other way.

I also came to realise that *Order and Love are the same thing*. We love people when we put them in an order, when we see them as children of God. It is when we see them as *things* that we do not love them. The thing that serves you your groceries or brings the food to your table, the coloured family who have depressed the value of your property by moving in next door, even the dear little child who delights you by her prettiness — the function, the effect, have come first — and there is no love. A woman who buys the best fillet steak for her poodle may think that she is showing love, but a dog should have the status of a dog. It is out of order, and therefore not love. A home of love is a home where there is order — not necessarily a complete absence of confusion, and not a home where everything is spick and span because things have become more important than people. Order means things in their *right* place, and then there is love.

X

I HAD LIVED IN SO MANY ROOMS and flats during my years in London that I thought nothing could surprise me. The drabness of Edinburgh shocked even me. The prevailing colour is brown, a nondescript muddy brown which pervades all the houses — as if, a hundred years ago, gallons and gallons of brown paint and hundreds of yards of brown furnishing material had been bequeathed, and Edinburgh citizens had been using it up ever since.

I arrived in Edinburgh in December and spent day after day going from one part of the city to another looking at rooms and flats each more depressing than the last. Edinburgh must be one network of railways, I thought, as again and again I found the place I had come to look at right on the railway. A pattern of small, uninteresting shaped rooms, with no outlook, noisy and smoky seemed to be endlessly repeated. Darkness fell in the early afternoon in the winter up here, but even in the so-called daylight it was murky and foggy with a continual drizzle of rain. My future here was an unknown quantity, and conditions were such as to make anyone thoroughly depressed. However, the opposite was the case, and I was filled with elation. Moments of happiness imprint themselves on the memory, and I can vividly recall coming out of church and stopping to buy a paper, and feeling a sudden flood of happiness and warmth towards all the passers-by.

For the first time I was establishing myself in a home. I had become aware of homes during my journey up England, and of their importance. They were part of establishing an existence as an individual. I had not been able to do that before, as I had not had the strength to live alone. Now I found that I had.

I was dimly beginning to realise, though I would not have expressed it thus, that, not being a wife or mother — that is a cell of a family unit — I myself had to be the family. Husband, wife, child — all these elements had to be contained within me. Six years ago I had known myself as half a thing; the other half had not come from outside, but had had to develop within my own nature.

To establish myself in a base had been my first concern. After a week's searching, I found myself in a pleasant residential district, entered a clean and well-kept house, and as soon as I came up to the top floor, which was to be let as an unfurnished flat, the contrast to all the other places I had seen was so apparent that I just heaved a sigh of relief — this was light and spacious and had character. As I stood looking out of the window where the Pentland Hills could be seen over the tops of the houses, the sun came out for the first time since I had arrived in Edinburgh and shone right into the room. I knew this was just the place to establish my home.

Buying furniture — a few new things, but most assembled from auction sales and secondhand shops — was a new experience. I knew the kind of things I wanted for my flat. It was to be a pleasant, cheerful place that anyone could come into and feel at home — no elegant drawing-room stuff for me; anyone, from a duchess to a dustman, should be able to be here without feeling, 'This is not the sort of place where I belong'. Harmony of colour was important, too. Gradually it built up. I worked hard to get the painting finished and then each day more pieces of furniture were delivered. It was as if they took a little time to get used to each other, and then settled down and became friends. With some carpeting on the floor, hiding the hideous linoleum and setting off the rugs which had been lent to me by my father, all became blended into a harmonious whole.

Lifting a large family Bible — one of the results of my auction sale shopping — from its place on the shelves, I settled down with it in front of the fire. To become familiar with the Bible was one of the things I had decided to do in Edinburgh, and I had bought a booklet prescribing daily reading for the purpose; embarking on this was one more solidity in a life that had been given solidity and an anchor by having my own things around me.

I had not intended to work inside the accountancy profession again. Yet here I was, a month after coming to Edinburgh, embarked on a new job, but it was not to last.

The other member of staff, a part-time typist, was also new; in fact we both started on the same day. The next day she gave in her notice. At the end of the week she was gone. That should have been a warning. It was not. A perfectionist in everything she did, my new employer's energy and drive knew no bounds. No hard-headed businessman could have been more ruthless in wringing out of people as much as possible for as little as possible. Gradually the pressure built up and my confidence plummeted. It became so that each day at the office was an ordeal to be faced, and it was not long before I was forced to look for a new job.

Having been constantly told how bad I was, my morale was given a necessary lift in my next office, where I was constantly told how good I was. McDonald and Fraser was a goodish firm with a goodish reputation which did the work that came its way. And for the first time in my life I found I was making a success of my job. Here I did not get on the wrong side of anybody. My responsibilities increased, and so did my salary. It was all part of settling down to an ordinary life as a solid citizen, and I was satisfied.

'These people just don't know what the *latihan* is', I felt when I joined the Subud group in Edinburgh. For I found here a very watered-down version of the strong force I had experienced at Coombe Springs. Subud, it seemed, was a force which was strong at the centre and gradually weakened as one went outwards. Edinburgh was very much on the periphery. But I noticed more differences between Subud in Edinburgh and Subud at Coombe Springs than the mere fact that the force of the *latihan* was weaker here.

In coming to Coombe Springs, Subud had come to a place where there was already a very strong feeling that we belonged one to another; 'the Work' had bound us by common experience and also by common awareness of its objective significance. Subud did not provide the common experience — in the *latihan* each person in the room fought his own battle, the nature of which the others were, necessarily, unaware — and the objective significance had altered, enlarged, for was not Subud to be for everyone? Just as we had come to take the *latihan* for granted as a necessity for spiritual hygiene, so we saw no reason to believe that it would not come to be so regarded by the population at large. Yet the future was still an unknown factor, both subjectively and objectively. We had these qualities — Submission, Surrender, Sincerity — constantly before us, but where were they leading us?

We could not know, because Subud had come to us so recently that we could not appraise it. Before, we had aimed at becoming conscious people, and had had some idea of what that had meant. Now we aimed at becoming purified people. But we had been told that at least three years must elapse before there was any chance of even the first stage of purification being accomplished. None of us had as yet been doing Subud for three years, so we could not see from our personal experience or from that of others around us where we were going. The only thing which could give us some clue was to look at Pak Subuh and those whom he had brought with him.

One result of becoming a purified person, it would seem, was that it made it much more difficult to live with the unpurified people of whom the rest of the world was composed; unpurified people gave off vibrations which purified people found hard to bear. When Pak Subuh started to give talks to Subud members during his first visit, he had immediately chosen a chair to sit in which had screened him on three sides, and the room had been arranged so that there was what someone had once described as a 'cordon sanitaire' of helpers between him and the main body of his audience. Harmful vibrations could also, apparently, enter into food, and one of the first changes to be made on the arrival of Pak Subuh and his party in 1957 was for the separate preparation of their food in their own quarters.

It was natural that we should look to Sjafrudin, a young Indonesian whom Pak Subuh left behind at the end of his first sojourn with us, when we asked ourselves, 'Where are we going?' He had been practising Subud for a number of years and was highly thought of by Pak Subuh. The effect on him might perhaps give us a clue. During his stay at Coombe Springs, Sjafrudin became more and more of a recluse — not through personal choice, but simply because the outside world became unbearable. Originally registered as a student, he had gone out each day to attend classes and had eaten his meals with the rest of us in the dining room. But the classes were soon given up, and so were the communal meals. If he ventured to the local store, for instance, it made him ill, and gradually he ventured out less and less, except when he was taken by car to one of the outlying centres for the *latihan*. Was *that* where we were headed?

The effect of Subud on us as individuals was an unknown quantity and so, it became increasingly clear, was Subud itself. Two of the women who were initially appointed helpers had been on a world tour, and had attended *latihan* with the women of Java. They gave us the impression that it was something of a very different order from the experience we knew. When, after three months' experience of the *latihan*, I had found I no longer resisted my impulses and was physically and vocally free, *that*, I had thought of the result, was the *latihan*; the quality of one's attention to this inner impulse and one's obedience in following it was what made a 'good exercise'. But there was more to it than that, as I had discovered on the last evening before Pak Subuh and his party left Coombe Springs after the 1959 Congress.

Ibu, Pak Subuh's wife, had been present that evening. Somehow I had become aware of her disapproval of the way I was speeding, faster and faster, round the edge of the room — the day had been a disturbing one for me and I had not arrived in a calm state — and it had come into my mind that there was nothing she could do to stop me. Then suddenly there she had been, right in front of me. She was a heavily-built woman and her bulk had completely blocked my path, though how it had got there I could not say. 'Stop' she had said, and I had stopped dead. Then I had collapsed on the seat that ran round the side of the hall. I had cried and cried — not the usual kind of tears that make you feel like a wet rag afterwards; this had been different, refreshing. So, so much, was being washed away by these tears. And Ibu had been there, stroking me. 'Now I know why you are called Ibu', I had thought, for she had seemed the eternal mother. 'I do not know what this has to do with Subud, or the worship of God', I had thought, 'but it is all very pleasant'.

The next time I had seen Ibu had been about two weeks later in Edinburgh. I had been unknown to her before, but she recognised me immediately. 'Now you exercise different', she had said. It had sounded like a command — but the whole point of the *latihan* was that there were no external commands and I had been puzzled. It had not been a command, though; it had been a statement. Never again did I have the impulse to move about in the *latihan* as before. Ibu's action had obviously had some effect, but I could not understand what had happened. How many people there must be, I thought, who were also in need of the kind of help I had received. And there was no one here who could give it to them.

Yes, there was more to the *latihan* than we had at first realised. And there was more to Subud than we had realised, too. We practised the *latihan* — the act of surrender — so that our lives might be an act of surrender. By the time I left Coombe Springs I had become aware of the potentialities of another, more direct way in which Subud could influence our lives to operate in accordance, not with our own wills, but with a greater Will. This was the practice of 'testing'.

Subud testing had been introduced to us by Pak Subuh not long after he had come to Coombe Springs, but it had been regarded then as quite an ancillary part of

Subud. But more and more emphasis was placed on the necessity of using this method in decision-making, and as we became more aware of the implications, we began to realise that it offered us a means of always knowing the right way in which to act. The method was this: a question would be asked, and those who were 'testing' would go into a state of *latihan* to 'receive' the answer. We were told to dismiss the question from our minds once it had been asked; an appropriate movement of the body, or sometimes an inner feeling, would indicate the answer to the question.

It had been obvious that the 1959 Congress would mark a new phase in the development of Subud, and by the time it was over it was clear that the keynote of this new phase was to be the practice of 'testing'. 'One cannot reach God with the mind' — if Subud could be said to have a 'message', it was this — and 'testing' took this precept a stage further. To know the right course of action, one simply laid one's mind on one side. All we knew about the future was that it would hold surprises. We did not know where we were going as individuals, we only knew we must submit to God's Will. The instrument of Subud also represented unknown potentialities which would develop — satisfactory results from 'testing' had been meagre, but they had not been negligible. Subud as a movement — we did not call it a movement, and the word is inappropriate for anything so passive, but I cannot think of a better one to describe its corporate existence as something which was evolving — the future of Subud in this sense was also unknown. However, to those of us who believed it played a part in human destiny, this was the aspect which had the most importance, and it was this we served.

This 'movement' had a unifying factor, and that was Pak Subuh himself. He might protest that he was not a leader, that that was not his role, but 'Bapak says . . .' was the final answer to anything. His lead was followed, even against the dictates of prudence and common sense, though with the passage of time the feeling increased that it was a case of the blind leading the blind. For what alternative was there?

We had learned in the course of the Subud Congress that Pak Subuh visualised the future of the Subud Brotherhood to consist of more than a collection of people who practised the *latihan*. He believed that Subud should function in the world through institutions, which would embrace humanitarian and commercial projects of all kinds. A Subud nursing home had, in fact, been inaugurated by him on his first visit; he had hoped that the Congress would result in many more schemes being initiated, and was particularly keen for a Subud school to be set up in this country. His ideal was that Subud members should work together at their ordinary life tasks, with professional men going into partnership, business men starting joint ventures etc. Then there would be little pools of people all over the world who worshipped God in this way and fulfilled their tasks in life; they would also, he said, prosper materially, and a proportion of the money would be available for charitable undertakings. In Indonesia, he had told us, there was a Subud bank, and when all the other banks had failed this one had managed to carry on.

None of this was of the slightest interest to the people I met for the *latihan* each Monday and Wednesday evening in a cold, damp and cheerless room underneath an Edinburgh church. They had not inherited and could not share a common past such as we had at Coombe Springs, and the present was merely the fact that they were there. Why were they there? Because, they believed, the result would be to purify and change their natures, and they sat back and waited for that day to dawn. Even the unifying element of taking a cue from Pak Subuh was absent here. Consequently it would have been useless to tell them that this approach did not accord with his view, or that on his second visit, although he had seen us with all our imperfections — and some of them must have horrified him — Pak Subuh had not told us to *wait* until this action of purification had taken place. Now, he had said, we could make our worship more pure by coming to the *latihan* in the right way, now we could begin to receive guidance for our actions, and that sentence which had burnt itself into my mind, *'every significant act is an act of worship'*, implied that now steps could be taken towards making our whole lives more acceptable to God.

Among the Subud members in Edinburgh, though, I found other migrants like myself who felt that they belonged to something, and were interested in the objective as well as the subjective value of Subud. And from a talk given by Mr Bennett during the course of a weekend he spent in Northumberland with Subud members from Scotland and the North of England, it was clear that the question of the significance of Subud for the world still continued to occupy his mind.

'All through the gospels', he said, 'comes the phrase, "He that hath eyes to see, let him see; he that hath ears to hear, let him hear".' But now, after two thousand years, people still did not have 'eyes to see and ears to hear'. So Subud had come, to give us just that. Hearing Mr Bennett speak like this, I reflected: three and a half years ago he had revealed to us that he had always regarded the work we had been doing — the exercises based on Gurdjieff's system — not as an end in itself, but as a preparation for something that was to come. Now once again, it seemed that he felt Subud itself was a preparation. Eyes to see what? Ears to hear what? He did not know, any more than we did.

XI

'WHY ARE THERE SO FEW people here to hear this?' I wondered as I looked round at the handful of people who had come to the Edinburgh headquarters of the Christian Community one evening. Adam Bittleston, the Priest there, had been comparing the different accounts of the Resurrection story in the four gospels. Was Mary Magdalene on her own or with the other Mary; was the stone rolled back by the angel or found already rolled back; were there two angels or one; was Jesus supposed by Mary Magdalene to be the gardener, or immediately recognised by her and the other Mary. Why did each account differ so much on the basic facts? We were not supplied with any glib answer; the object had been to provoke thought. I had had no idea that such paradoxes existed, and to face such a puzzlement was just the sort of way I wanted to spend my time. I went home content with my evening.

As soon as I had felt myself established in Edinburgh, I had begun to look around. I had left the secluded world of Coombe Springs for the larger world outside, and wanted to know more of this world and its streams of thought, and to pursue further the ideas which the time at Kitty's had merely introduced me to. *'Pray for wisdom and understanding'*, I had been told. God could give me the wisdom to understand, but the raw material on which this God-given power was to work — that I had to find for myself.

Kitty had been anxious about my coming to Edinburgh, feeling that I needed help and guidance the Subud group there could not supply. She had impressed on me that the Christian Community had a thriving branch and gave me an introduction to Adam Bittleston, who was a personal friend of hers.

The teachings of Rudolph Steiner had been very important to the formation of Kitty's ideas, and she attached great importance to the work of the Christian Community, founded according to his principles. So it was natural that one of the first things I should have done in this process of outward-looking was to turn my steps in this direction.

There was undoubtedly something special here, which struck me when I entered the small chapel one day when it was empty. I did not know what the shapes of the objects on the altar signified, but I felt that it was good, wholesome. Most of the people I met at the Christian Community were anthroposophists, as Rudolph Steiner's followers are called. Later, attending any meeting at which a number of them were present, I could pick out at a glance who, among the audience, were anthroposophists. They had a quality which I can only describe as 'precious'. It struck me that this was not, and never would be, the main stream. No, it was not here, or in any such minority group, that I felt I should be.

It was the Church to which I turned, because I felt I wanted to worship God with ordinary people. The Church, I found, played a much larger part in the life of the community here than in England, and in the Church of Scotland I found myself at the centre of religious life.

I found in it the simplicity that had appealed to me in the Nonconformist Churches in England, and the position of the minister, that is, not someone who comes between you and God like a priest, but a simple servant, seemed very right. Doctrinal differences I did not go into, because I knew that with no denomination would I wholly agree. At one time this had kept me away from church, but now I felt that the important thing was to worship God with my fellows, and that my reservations were of secondary importance. Besides, there was much less now that I could not accept. There was really only one word in the Apostles' Creed I could not say — the word 'only': 'And in Jesus Christ, His *only* Son our Lord.' I sensed that there was some significance in Christ which I had missed and which was important. But the word 'only' implied that the world was composed of Christians and Infidels. The universality in my spiritual training repelled me from *that*. Gurdjieff taught that all the Founders of Religion had been Messengers from God, and Pak Subuh, being a Muslim, spoke of the Prophet Moses, the Prophet Jesus, and the Prophet Muhammad as though they were all the same.

I became a member of the congregation of a church round the corner from my flat. Knowing nothing of the district, I had gone there initially because it was the nearest, and it turned out to be a fortunate choice. The minister was young and inspiring — a really dedicated man — and I found, coming to a service here, that it was not a dead thing, but true worship. However, I considered that it was only because I had had the awakening of Subud that I was able to find it here.

I wanted to enter into the life of the church, so as well as attending its services I also attended social and other functions. Later I joined one of the Bible study groups and met fortnightly with about ten other members of the congregation in the home of one of the Elders. I enjoyed these evenings. The group consisted of good sincere people, who had everything except the vital spark to set it all alight. I could not have talked to them about Subud; there was no way of saying what it could give, but I did wish that it could come to people like this, because I felt that they would use the Force aright; that then it would be like high grade petrol in high grade cars.

Though I regarded Subud as the centre of my spiritual life, my point of contact with God, and the path along which lay my way towards living a life in accordance with His Will, nevertheless the Sunday services at the local church came to mean a great deal to me. To be one of the congregation following the minister in prayer, the whole pattern of the service — yes, that hour was a holy time in the simple and joyful sense of the word. And when it came to Communion Sunday — four times a year in the Church of Scotland — that really was a celebration.

My forays into the Christian world were not confined to the local church. Walking down one of the streets in my neighbourhood one day, I saw a church-like building with a notice board outside. 'St Ninian's Conference and Training Centre (Interdenominational)' I read at the top of the notice board. Underneath were details of activities at which, it said, all would be welcome. I made a note of these, and in due course was attending a number of activities here.

I liked what I found in this place. The atmosphere was somewhat reminiscent of Coombe Springs in that everyone pitched in to do what was needed, and I came to have a great admiration for the Reverend D. P. Thomson, the guiding light of the whole enterprise, who reminded me of Mr Bennett. He gave the impression that every breath he took, every action he made was as a Christian. No longer young and suffering from heart trouble, he had immense vitality and enthusiasm, and his joy of life affected everyone. Though obviously possessing great learning, he never allowed this to intrude or impede the spirit which flowed through him. He was not a man ever to let things stand still — he always had some new scheme on hand, and as soon as that was launched another would follow.

The people who came to Fountainhall Road seemed to be very much of a type — most of them had grown up in Christian families, gone to Sunday School as children and continued going to church ever since. They were either happily married or still living at home, and generally were people with whom life had dealt kindly. I did not feel they were here as a result of any struggle, that there had ever been burning questions in their minds. At first it had felt like Coombe Springs, but really it was very different. Most of the people at Coombe Springs had had an unhappy life but were struggling upwards and had come because they were searching.

I found myself in a base for taking Christianity out to the world and I began to feel hypocritical. I wanted to continue coming, because I felt that here I might learn something. I was still convinced that if I could really understand the role of Christ, I would have the key to what I needed. Despite this conviction, my reservations grew. In the general Christian attitude there was so much that did not make sense to me, so much that was sentimental. The fact that Christ's death was given central significance — 'Jesus Christ Who died for us' — was extremely puzzling to me. That such a Being lived on this earth was significant. His death must surely have been a release. Much as I might like to be, I was only too aware that I was not a Christian in the sense that those who came to Fountainhall Road were Christians.

One more Christian experience, of a very different kind, might be mentioned here. When I had been on holiday in the Tyrol in 1958, an excursion had included a visit to Oberammergau, the Bavarian village where the Passion Play is performed every ten years. I had promised myself that when it was next performed I would go. It was now 1960, and I kept the promise. I did not tell many people about my trip, for to most it would seem crazy to go all that way to spend eight hours — four in the morning and four in the afternoon — sitting on a hard wooden seat in the cold watching an amateur performance in a language I did not understand. In the event, it was something very special. Even the technical quality was far above what can be seen on the West End stage, and as for the spirit of it — surely these people would never be the same again.

This little village, though visited, even in ordinary years, by many tourists, had retained its purity; an oasis unsullied by the world. The many visitors had come with a common purpose. The play was not a spectacle; it was an act of worship, for players and spectators alike, and the communion service on the eve of the performance was not a separate event, but part of the whole. So was all of the two days spent in the village, and my last act, the purchase of a wood-carving.

If I had not known in any other way that here was a people devoted to God, I would have known it by the quality of the wood-carving which was the main 'industry' of the village. It was this that had captivated my attention on my first visit two years previously and I had marvelled at the living quality which had somehow been instilled into the figures carved by the masters — there was no mistaking which were theirs and which their pupils, though I had not been able to put my finger on any difference. I had resolved that when I came to the play I would buy one.

Now I had come, and I had brought money for a wood-carving with me. There was one which stood out. 'Yes, that is my favourite', said the carver. Most of the others were conventional figures of Christ or of saints.

This was of Christ crucified, but instead of being on a cross, He was surrounded by something that seemed to be unfolding and He was emerging. I felt that this expressed Christ in this New Age — He should not still be on a cross.

I had become more and more fond of Edinburgh. I had not realised that in coming here I would literally be living in another country — Lossiemouth, though further north geographically, had been much closer to England culturally. The pace of life here was much slower, and there was also a feeling of solidity, of people belonging, for most of the shops outside the centre were one-man businesses. I was always aware of the physical structure of Edinburgh. I was living not in a two-dimensional city but in a three-dimensional one; I could be at street level, and four floors lower down still be at street level. After the vastness of London, it was a welcome contrast to live in a city where nowhere was more than ten minutes away by car, and there were all sorts of cross-links whereby the same people turned up in different connections.

Wherever I went in England I had, particularly in my voice, the stamp of the sort of background I had come from. In Edinburgh this was not so — to the man in the street I was just 'English'. Another great relief.

I was not even sorry that I had come to a place with a rather stagnant Subud group, for otherwise I might not have had as much time and energy to look round at some of the other things that were going on in the world. There was no doubt that a great wakening-up process was taking place and could be seen in many fields. For so long most of my attention had been on only one of these streams; now I was taking a broader and wider look.

My contact with the Church had convinced me that it, too, was feeling the new life that was coming into the world. But always there, I had my reservations. Around Christmas time there had been much talk of the Incarnation, and this whole concept was unreal to me. I still felt that it was important to understand the role of Christ, that without this something was missing, but the key to understanding it was not in the emphasis the Church put upon it. But then I was not so sure, as every day, passing a certain church, I was faced with the text: 'I am the Way, the Truth, and the Life; no man cometh to the Father but by Me.' It seemed that this was not the Church but Christ Himself saying that only Christians went to heaven. But I knew that could not be true; there must be millions of people in the world who had 'come to the Father' by means of other religions and ways. It was very puzzling.

I was out in the world again, and I was getting the feel of it. I could feel life bubbling up all round me, and always there were surprises. I went to many meetings, and the audiences interested me as much as the speakers. I was outraged on one occasion, by both. The speaker felt his missionary hospital in a Muslim country to be a little Christian oasis among all the heathens that surrounded him. Speaking of the Islamic belief: 'There is no God but God and Muhammad is His Prophet', he asserted that a

Christian could not accept either part! Their idea of God was not the same as our idea of God. I felt outraged. Did not Muslims regard God as the supreme Creator the same as we did? How could there be any difference? As I looked round the room, I saw no one who felt as I did. I felt like rushing off to the nearest mosque.

On the other hand, the audience who came to hear the Maharishi Mahesh Yogi on his visit to Edinburgh belied any assertion that Edinburgh was spiritually narrow or dead. Thoughtful and searching questions followed his talk. For myself, as soon as the Maharishi started to speak, I forgot the irritation of the stage-management which had aimed to give an air of Eastern mystery. He was such a good example of his own philosophy. The time had now come, he said, when everyone should be happy, and there is no doubt about it, he was happy — I have never seen a person whom one knew so definitely to be happy. The key to it all was his 'simple method of meditation' which he was willing to impart to anyone who wished. The Edinburgh audience, however, did not easily accept that suffering could have no place in the scheme of things.

The idea of myself asking to be initiated into his 'simple method of meditation' was something I did not even consider. I was interested in knowing what was going on in the world, but I was not looking for anything to take part in. For was I not, by means of Subud, training to become rendered to God's will — and how could there be a substitute for that?

I had often heard Kitty speak of Dr Heidenreich, whom she used to visit at the Christian Community headquarters in London, so when I heard he was to come and give a talk on Rudolph Steiner to mark the centenary of his birth, I went to hear him. From this I received more idea of Steiner himself than I had ever had before. He must, I thought, like Gurdjieff and other teachers, have been of great value in his own lifetime. But afterwards it all seems to turn into something quite different from what the author intended. Watching the people come in, I could pick out the Steiner ones, and again I felt they were out of the main stream.

Seeing a notice in the paper one day, I thought here was something of interest I would go to. It was headed 'World Religion Day' and there were to be speakers on the Jewish, Christian, Muslim and Bahá'í faiths. Jewish, Christian, Muslim, yes, but what was Bahá'í? Who was organising it, anyway? I looked more closely and saw at the top 'Bahá'í World Faith'. So these people were setting themselves up as just as important as the Jews, Christians and Muslims? What a nerve! But anyway it would be interesting to hear the other three, and I would go.

I found the room full and people standing, but managed to slip into a vacant seat. It was all quite interesting. The Jew spoke of some of the rites and obligations of his religion, which I listened to with interest as I have always had a respect for the Jewish Faith. I was rather ashamed of the Christian, a stage parson who certainly showed himself to be the most prejudiced. I do not remember much about the Muslim. The Bahá'í said something about a later revelation — a continuation of the line of Prophets after Muhammad. 'But has no one ever told him that Muhammad was the last?' I wondered, for the doctrine that Muhammad's title, 'The Seal of the Prophets', meant that the prophetic line ended with Him was one I had never questioned.

The meeting, I felt, had been worth coming to. On the way out I stopped at the bookstall. Someone picked up one of the books and advised me to read it, and before I knew where I was I was walking away having bought it.

It so happened that soon after this meeting I went to stay a few weeks at my father's house. He and my stepmother were away and their housekeeper was nervous of being left on her own. My usual evening activities were therefore curtailed, and I had time to read the book I had bought: *Bahá'u'lláh and the New Era* by J.E.Esslemont. I did not even know how to pronounce it, but I read it through, and was relieved to find it contained so much sense.

Its teachings about Life after Death and the different stages of existence particularly attracted me. It seemed to put everything into perspective. As life in the womb is to life after birth, it said, so this life is to the fuller life which commences at so-called death. And just as an embryo in the womb cannot understand what it is like to see and eat and move about and do all the other hundred-and-one things that a person in this world does, so one cannot possibly conceive of the fuller life that one will enter when one is born into the next world. It was a simple analogy, but it confirmed all that I had learned over the year, in stressing the importance of this life not for its own sake but for the sake of what was to come after. My interest was aroused.

XII

IT WAS TWO MONTHS AFTER the World Religion Day meeting that I saw another notice in the paper under the heading 'Bahá'í World Faith'. This time it was advertising a talk explaining the Bahá'í Faith itself. I decided I would go.

As soon as the speaker began, I knew that I was going to find a mixture of common sense, no-nonsense and humour much to my liking. His opening words took me back four years to a series of lectures Mr Bennett had given then. A scale of orders of being had been put forward from a crystal up through plant, animal, human, etc and the place of each in the scheme of things postulated. Now the speaker was explaining how, just as a tree could not know what it was like to be an animal — to see, to hear, to move about — and an animal could not know what it was like to be human, so a human, when faced with a Being of a higher order, had not the apparatus to comprehend it. He then spoke of an order of beings having our attributes but something more as well, just as a human has the attributes of an animal in addition to more developed mental and spiritual facilities, and called them Manifestations of God. Such were Jesus, Muhammad, Moses, and others. They had a special function with regard to mankind. He used the analogy of school teachers.

At each stage of a child's development, she needs lessons commensurate with her understanding. The time comes when she must move into another class, to learn more advanced lessons from another teacher. None of these teachers is greater than the other — the teacher of the infant class is quite capable of teaching differential calculus, but of course would not dream of doing so. Unfortunately, by the time the new teacher comes, the child has got so attached to the personality of her old one that she cannot accept that the new one, with strange, new ideas and a different approach, comes from the same source. So it is with these Manifestations of God, each of whom is sent into the world with a specific message relative to the time and place to which He comes. Rivalry between the followers of the different religions ensues, each claiming that their teacher has revealed the final and absolute truth and refusing to listen to any other.

So far, I had heard nothing radically different from what I already believed. Mr Bennett also talked of an educative process of humanity — that mankind if left to itself would just degenerate, but that from time to time an influence comes from outside which brings it up to a higher level — but he was not so specific as to its nature. From here, though, they parted company. In Mr Bennett's view the human race was still in its infancy, but the

Bahá'ís presented a different hypothesis. I really began to sit up and take notice.

The present time was, we were told, a crucial one in the history of mankind. For mankind — and this I found scarcely credible — was on the threshold of maturity. The time had come for us all to progress from our parochial schools — the Christian in one part of the world, the Buddhist in another, and so on — and enter one big University. In this University, we would find followers of different curricula, adding to the richness. We now had to learn how to take our places as adult citizens of a mature world. He then went on to speak of these Beings whose coming initiated a New Age.

The next thing he said was a big shock. I had quite come to accept that we were on the threshold of a New Age, maybe that it had already dawned — certainly I placed its inception in the present century. That was not what this man said. He told us that the dawn of the New Age was in the nineteenth century, when the Manifestation of God, the Educator for this Age, had made His appearance. Surely this could not be true. That an event of this magnitude had occurred more than a century ago and I had not heard of it seemed incredible. Still, I would listen to what else he had to say.

The time we are now living in, he said, was so crucial in the history of mankind that God had thought fit to send us not one Manifestation of God, but two! Bahá'u'lláh — that name I had not known how to pronounce, whose accent comes on the second and fourth syllables — had revealed the teachings and laws under which mankind was to live for the next thousand years.

The one who had paved the way for Him, as John the Baptist had for Jesus, was also a Manifestation of God in His own right, called the Báb.

Each Manifestation of God renewed the eternal message of Religion; each time we were enjoined to love, honesty, purity etc. Hand in hand with the eternal message was always a specific one suited to the time and place in which the Manifestation of God came. The laws and ordinances of religion — the social teachings — were thus changed according to the needs of the age. Also signs were given by which future Manifestations of God could be recognised.

The particular message of Bahá'u'lláh was centred round the notion that the world was now *one world*. We had never before needed teachings on how to live in a world that was one world. We did now, and Bahá'u'lláh had given them to us.

He then spoke of the mission of Christ. He too had brought a renewal of the eternal Religion, teachings for His day, and signs by which the Manifestation of God who would appear 'in the latter days' would be recognised. Unlike Moses, who came before Him, He was not really concerned with specific laws and ordinances — the only two that the gospels record Him concerning Himself with are the Sabbath and divorce. The emphasis was different. He could see the time approaching when mankind would come into its own. 'The Kingdom of Heaven is upon you', He said, and a part of His mission was to prepare us for this day. He gave signs by which men could recognise its coming, that they might watch for One who would come 'as a thief in the night'.

As I listened to this man speaking, it was not like hearing something new, but as though I had been straining to look down a telescope and seen everything all blurred, and he had come along and twiddled the eye piece and everything had come into focus. Yet I wondered what authority he had for saying all this.

It was all in the teachings of Bahá'u'lláh. In 1863, Bahá'u'lláh had proclaimed that He was a Manifestation of God, that He spoke with the Voice of God. He had made the very highest claim that it is possible to make. It was either true or false. This man had accepted that it was true; so had a number of other people in the room. They believed, therefore, that everything the speaker had said had come from God.

We were told that if we came back at half-past seven that evening, we could talk more informally and ask any further questions. The meeting ended; the woman beside me had also been impressed, but the rest of the audience had consisted largely of stolid Scottish women who had sat staunch and unyielding throughout. The speaker had been quite humorous, really, but not a glimmer had I seen on any of their faces.

When I went to church that evening I sat near the door and slipped out before the end of the service so as to be back at the George Hotel by half-past seven. We gathered round in a small circle to share our thoughts and raise any questions we might have.

I hoped they wouldn't think I wasn't interested, but really there was no question I could ask. Three and a half years ago I had become committed to a life lived, as far as possible, in accordance with God's Will. And the signposts directing me along that path had been the three words: Surrender, Submission, Sincerity. If I was to continue to be guided by these precepts, then there was only one question: *Is it true*? Bahá'u'lláh had claimed that His word was the Word of God, and that His commands were Divine commands to mankind, valid for at least a thousand years, and until I resolved this question, everything else was irrelevant. In Subud I was undergoing a training for the purpose of becoming submissive to God's Will, but if Bahá'u'lláh really had been a Divine Mouthpiece; if, through Him, we really had been *told* what to do, then I could not ignore it. If I did, I would be denying the very thing I professed to live by. These people believed that Bahá'u'lláh's claim was valid, so there was at least a chance it might be.

We learned of the life of Bahá'u'lláh. He did not sound like someone who made extravagant claims for personal advantage or for self-aggrandizement. A lifetime of persecution, exile and imprisonment was the sole reward for his pains. He could have had a life of ease, wealth and temporal power. Perhaps He was under some sort of delusion. It did not sound like that either. We were thrown back on what seemed the only alternative — incredible as it might be — that it was true. But why had nobody ever told me before?

When a Manifestation of God comes into the world, God does not give him a passport with MANIFESTATION OF GOD written in large letters so that everyone will know who He is and that His word is the Word of God. To outward appearances He is just like other men, but God has made provision whereby He can be recognised — in the prophecies given by earlier Manifestations of God and by the lesser prophets. The scriptures of all the religions foretell the coming of Bahá'u'lláh. The Bible is full of prophecies concerning Him. The word Bahá'u'lláh translated into English means 'Glory of God'. All through the Old Testament there are references to 'The Glory of God', 'The Glory of the Father', etc. Christ described Bahá'u'lláh sometimes as the Spirit of Truth, sometimes in terms of His own return. I had never thought much about prophecy before, but obviously it had been given to us for a purpose. I must go back to my Bible, I thought, and see how I felt in the light of all this.

So again I was brought face to face with the possibility that Bahá'u'lláh really was who He said He was. 'He lived a perfect life; He brought Divine teachings for mankind; He fulfilled the prophecies', said our speaker. What more proof did we need?

Some people asked questions about what was involved in being a Bahá'í. It was interesting to hear about their personal conduct, their relationships with one another, but I felt all this was beside the point. If Bahá'u'lláh had really spoken with the voice of God, then whatever He said one would have to do. If I had heard that Bahá'ís spent three hours a day standing on their heads, it would not have affected the issue.

The Bahá'í Faith was referred to as a faith rather than a religion. There was only one God, so there could only be one Religion, which all the Divine Messengers had come to reveal. Before he can become a Bahá'í, a Jew must accept Christ and a Christian must accept Muhammad. We talked about evolution, and again my ideas came into focus. There *was* evolution, but I had not understood how anyone could support Darwin's theory of Natural Selection. The Bahá'í teaching was that man had always been man. Although he might have evolved through a fish-like form, a monkey-like form, and so on, the potentiality of becoming a man had always been latent within him, as the potentiality of becoming an oak tree is latent within the acorn. This made a lot of sense to me.

And the biblical text I had found myself so unable to reconcile: 'I am the Way, the Truth and the Life, no man cometh to the Father but by Me' — that mystery, too, was cleared up. Christ was not denying the validity of other religions, but asserting that it is the Manifestation of God Who is the contact between God and the people on earth. In Christ's day, many people had claimed such a station and offered a way to find God. Christ had negated this.

It was not just on theological questions that my ideas began to crystallise. Bahá'u'lláh had also revealed laws for society, and I found in the social teachings — which would influence both individual and collective life — much to interest me. For years and years I had seen that none of the political systems practised in any part of the world could give society the government it needed. Maybe there was hope here too in the spiritual principles that were to govern mankind's social and political affairs.

Our speaker read a prayer to end the meeting, and as he did so, his voice seemed to come from inside me. It was an extraordinary experience, and one I have never had before or since. I went home. I had been challenged. Nothing was more important now than to satisfy myself, beyond any doubt, of the answer to the question 'Is it true?' But already, in my heart, I knew that it was.

PART THREE

'The true seeker hunteth naught but the object of his quest.'

From *The Seven Valleys*

XIII

I WENT TO THE LIBRARY the day after the meeting at the George Hotel and took out a book on the Bahá'í Faith called *All Things Made New* by John Ferraby.

I am usually very bad at waking up in the morning, and it is as much as I can do — very often more than I can do — to get to work on time. Every morning of this week, at about six o'clock, I was wide awake and reaching for the book. At lunch-time I would make a dash for the nearest restaurant where I could read peacefully, and I wanted to do nothing each evening except fly back home and read again. It was a long book, and each page would have merited pondering over. But I gulped it up and by the end of the week it was finished.

It was like looking at an architect's plans for a house that one knows one will live in. I knew this was where I was going to end up. I could not resist turning first to one of the later chapters, entitled 'Laws, Obligations and Teaching the Faith'. Would I one day be doing these things, I wondered — reciting certain 'obligatory prayers' every day and for nineteen days in the year fasting from sunrise to sunset, guarding my tongue from all backbiting and calumny, regarding my work as a form of worship, abstaining from alcohol, and when I died being buried instead of cremated?

I read the stories of these two Manifestations of God who had followed each other in such swift succession: the Báb, young, gentle, courteous, radiating such love that all who came within His orbit were overcome by it. Brought before the divines and notables of the city of Tabriz, He had declared, 'I am, I am, I am the Promised One! I am the One Whose name you have for a thousand years invoked, at Whose mention you have risen, Whose advent you have longed to witness, and the hour of Whose Revelation you have prayed to God to hasten. Verily, I say, it is incumbent upon the peoples of both the East and the West to obey My word, and to pledge allegiance to My person. (See *All Things Made New*, p. 192.)

After six years — a large part of it spent in prison — the Báb was martyred; and was there ever such a dramatic story as the circumstances of His martyrdom? But neither exile, imprisonment nor death had stemmed the flow of thousands upon thousands of people — the rich and the poor, the simple and unlettered and the most learned in the land — who had come forward to embrace His cause. No fewer than twenty thousand of them had joyfully suffered martyrdom in the most brutal and barbaric circumstances.

Bahá'u'lláh, on the other hand, had been called upon to endure a lifetime of suffering. Again, I received the impression of a spirit unbowed by the tribulations heaped upon Him, of power and majesty shining through the outward conditions of degradation and poverty. When I read of Him, as a prisoner, addressing the rulers of the earth with these words: 'Ye are but vassals, 0 kings of the earth! He Who is the King of Kings hath appeared, arrayed in His most wondrous glory, and is summoning you unto Himself' they seemed only fitting. Bahá'u'lláh had sent exhortations to individual rulers and divines and to many groups of people throughout the world. He had told them, clearly, what was required of them. After reading of so much that had happened in Persia and such-like exotic places, it was a relief to read of such a letter sent to Queen Victoria. I was pleased that, unlike most of the others, she had not rejected it out of hand saying that if it was of God, it would endure. Warnings had been sent to leaders such as Napoleon III, then at the height of his power, saying that unless he arose to help this Cause, his kingdom would be thrown into confusion, and his empire pass from his hands. One by one, the prophecies contained in these warnings came to pass.

Bahá'u'lláh, I found, had brought far more to the world than a code of laws. He had brought a blueprint for a transformed civilisation. The book concluded with the idea of Universal Cycles. For the first few thousand years of a Universal Cycle, successive Manifestations of God guide mankind to greater spiritual maturity. When the time is ripe, a Universal Manifestation appears and mankind enters an Age of Fulfilment, lasting for some hundreds of thousands of years. All through the present Universal Cycle, the Prophets have looked to the Day of the Universal Manifestation, Bahá'u'lláh, when the world would become 'one fold with one shepherd'.

From this book, I glimpsed an emerging world where the teachings of Bahá'u'lláh were universally accepted. I also glimpsed what life was like now for those who had accepted Bahá'u'lláh and called themselves Bahá'ís.

XIV

A DOZEN OR SO PEOPLE meeting together in someone's sitting room, with prayers, readings, perhaps a discussion, followed by general conversation over a cup of tea — coming amongst the Bahá'ís in this way, I was amazed at the contrast between what I felt here and what I had felt at the Bible study group or at any of the other activities connected with the Church. I had become convinced that people who had not had the advantage of the Subud 'opening' were missing something. With the Bahá'ís I felt none of this, that indefinable 'spiritual vitality' was evident here, too. In the *latihan* 'something happened' which could not be explained. Something also happened here, no less potent for its having no outward manifestation. I would have to leave my superiority complex behind.

I knew Bahá'u'lláh had lived a perfect life and that he had fulfilled the prophecies. One more thing would prove to me that Bahá'u'lláh's claim was a valid one, and that is summed up in Christ's warning against false prophets: 'By their fruits ye shall know them.' I was now tasting the 'fruits'. Nothing could have impressed me more than this Life of the Spirit I found here.

Little by little I was coming to the inescapable answer to my question, 'Is it true?' I knew a time would come when I could evade it no longer, but I was in no hurry — I knew it would mean my life would never be the same again.

Side by side with my growing satisfaction with my Sunday evenings among the Bahá'ís, I was gradually finding that when I went to the *latihan*, the whole thing was drying up. I still continued to go regularly, but each time it meant less. After about ten minutes time began to drag. Subud still had far more than a personal significance for me. I had never doubted its objective value in the world, so that I regarded service to Subud as service to humanity. At Coombe Springs I had watched its growth from day to day, and in Edinburgh, as one of a very small nucleus attending regularly, I felt some responsibility. So in spite of this drying-up process, I continued to attend.

The time came, though, when I realised there must be a balance between giving and receiving, and to go merely for the sake of duty would be artificial and unreal. It was no more right than it was to go for benefit without any idea of service. I tried to explain my position to Eileen, one of the helpers. I was in the greatest turmoil. I told her how my world had been turned upside down since hearing of the Bahá'í Faith, and at least for the time being I would not be coming to the *latihan*. Maybe when this turmoil had subsided I would feel I could start coming again. Although I said this, we both knew that I would not start coming again, and that Subud was something in my life that was now of the past.

In answer to her natural curiosity, I told Eileen of the spirit I had found among the Bahá'ís and she agreed that there were places where one was conscious of a force, as one was conscious of a force in Subud. She asked if I had anything she could read, and left with a book.

Speaking of the spirit found among the Bahá'í's, I meant more than the presence of the 'spiritual vitality' I had found absent in Christian circles. A force was present, as it was in the *latihan*, but I soon became aware of one very big difference: the force among the Bahá'ís was a cohesive one, it brought them into relationship with one another, and all who came within their orbit also felt a part of the whole. Long before I sorted out names and faces, I had been conscious of a oneness with them. This was absent in Subud, where each one of us was an island.

I had not yet embarked upon the regular daily prayer and other spiritual disciplines of the Bahá'ís, and wondered if I was being premature in letting go of the rope. It seemed so. Like all periods of transition, it was extremely uncomfortable. Falling in love is always uncomfortable. The transition from the state of not loving to the state of loving is never easy, and this was like that only much worse. It affected everything. I had been in the process of settling down and was happy with my life. I had not wanted anything to come along and disturb my peace. True, I had wanted to understand, but I had not bargained for being shaken to the foundations as a result.

At the Sunday evening meetings, I was learning more about this Faith, and things came into perspective. Initially it was Bahá'u'lláh's claim that had arrested my attention. 'Is he or isn't he?' was the only question. The next thing to investigate had been His message, and I took more interest in how, He said, the world could live together in harmony and peace, in the World Government He envisaged and how it was to come about, as well as His personal teachings.

There is a difference between when a Bahá'í talks about his Faith, and when, for instance, a Christian talks about his. Most Christians I know feel free to take or reject what they want from their Church with the exception, perhaps, of Roman Catholics. Generally speaking, when a Christian talks of his Faith he is speaking of a personal thing — belief in God, belief in Christ, the endeavour to live a Christ-like life. When a Bahá'í talks about his Faith it includes everything to do with being a Bahá'í - belief in Bahá'u'lláh as a Manifestation of God; living a life according to His precepts; all the social and spiritual principles to ensure an organised, united body of believers. All this was an equally essential part of the Faith of a Bahá'í.

If Christ had said in clear and unambiguous language that Peter was to be the first Pope; had outlined precisely his functions and how his successors were to be appointed; if these instructions had been recorded and their authenticity could be proved beyond doubt; if successors had been appointed in accordance with the instructions and there was an unblemished record of their conduct down the ages, then Christians could all turn to a central point of authority, and if they did not they would be disobeying the injunctions of Christ.

This is the position of the Bahá'í. It is his Faith that when Bahá'u'lláh spoke, it is as though God were speaking, and not to obey is to disobey God. Since there is so much, all fully authenticated, that Bahá'u'lláh did say, in every department of his life he has the chance to live as a Bahá'í. Just as he has no doubt of Bahá'u'lláh's injunctions regarding prayer and fasting, he has no doubt about his place in the organic life of the Bahá'í community, an equally essential part of his Faith.

My discomfort increased throughout this period and I found myself open, sensitive and vulnerable. As at all times when a change is taking place within one, I seemed to be in a state of plasticity; even my body no longer felt set hard into its mould, but became soft and pliable as the body of a woman becomes more pliable when she is pregnant. I could not concentrate on my work, for just as one might feel that every moment away from a lover is a moment wasted, so had I come to feel about the Bahá'ís. This was quite impersonal — whether any particular person was there or not was immaterial; when I was with the Bahá'ís I was at peace with the world.

XV

I REALLY HAD TO TAKE MYSELF TO TASK. Three months ago I had heard the ring of truth among the Bahá'ís. Now I could no longer summon up any shred of doubt that this was the way that God had manifested Himself to mankind in this age, and anyone professing a willingness to do the Will of God could not ignore it. But was I really so sure? Can there ever be anything of which one is certain? Our minds are only finite. Was I not just too gullible?

All the same, a tremendous pressure was building up within me, and when sleepless night after sleepless night was followed by a day when I had not found it possible to get to the office at all, I knew the decision could be put off no longer. In the evening in my flat, I sat down to write a simple declaration of faith that would formally signify my belief in Bahá'u'lláh and my wish to be received into the Bahá'í Community.

As I was about to pick up my pen, there was a knock on the front door. I opened it to find the black-coated, dog-collared figure of a minister outside. I asked him in. He was calling on all the flats in the block to find out which of the tenants would be members of his church and which had other affiliations. I had not expected, after deciding that the time had come to stand up to the world and say, 'I am a Bahá'í', that the first opportunity would come so soon.

One of the features of life as a Bahá'í is the daily obligatory prayer. Prayer is the one thing which, all down the ages, has been proclaimed as indispensable to the life of the spirit. To accept its necessity, and to get down to it, are two different things. There is only one way to learn to pray, and that is to do it. I had to learn to do it.

Taking up my life in Edinburgh as a Bahá'í, a great light shone. When, years ago, I had been in love for the first time, everything around me had taken on an extraordinary vividness. It was like that now, only greatly intensified. Four times a day I walked through Princes Street Gardens on my way to or from the office, and each time I saw the flowers, the birds, the fountains, the beautiful shape of St Cuthbert's Kirk, all anew. When a rabbit popped its head out from behind a hedge it was as though I had never seen a rabbit before. I was the same old person but within this thirty-five-year-old body dwelt a new-born baby. Why everything should be transformed because I had accepted the Faith of Bahá'u'lláh I could not understand. I only knew that I now walked in the light where previously I had walked in darkness.

'Exciting, isn't it?' someone had said when told I had

recently made my declaration of faith. I thought for a moment. 'No, not exciting', I said. 'Just a relief, really.' Of course it had been a relief on a personal level, an end to the indecision, to the conflict between the inner pressure and the outer 'sensible self'. It was also a relief that, after all, God was in charge. It was a relief to look at the world, which had seemed so topsy-turvy, and see that, after all, all was in order and going to plan.

With the wonder of it all upon me, I would look at people and wish they could know what I knew. Some people in particular I wished I had a way to tell. Every morning when I left the flat two workmen working in the Court were sitting in their little shelter having a cup of tea. All I could say as I passed was 'Good morning'. There was a reality in them and the 'good morning' was a real exchange between human beings. I wished I could convey to them what had happened and was happening. But we did not even speak the same language.

I did have a common language with Eileen, not only of dialect, but of terms to express abstract ideas. Yet I had not been able to convey the magnitude of what had occurred to her either. I felt exasperated when she passed up an opportunity to meet a visiting Bahá'í speaker because it was her Subud evening. It seemed as though I had told a blind man he would have a chance of recovering his sight, but he preferred to go to his braille class. Braille is a very good thing for the sight-impaired, and Subud a great help to those groping in the dark. *But there is no need to be in the dark.* Not only is there light, but also a map to find the way.

XVI

'IF THIS IS TRUE, then it is the most important thing I have ever heard', I had realised on that fateful day when I had gone to hear what the Bahá'í Faith was all about; 'and yet, until now, nobody has ever told me'. Now the tables were turned; if I did not do something about it the accusation could be levelled against me: 'You knew, and you never told us'.

While Bahá'ís are not allowed to proselytize and try to avoid confrontational religious argument, each is none the less enjoined to 'teach the Faith', to share information about their religion with any who seek it. There is, of course, a fine line between sharing truth in a spirit of friendship and pressing one's views on others, but for myself, I felt obliged to share my findings with those who had been my companions on the Way. To our group which had met at Coombe Springs from 1954 to 1957, we had each brought our measure — anything which affected our inner life, we had been told, was relevant, and should be contributed to the pool to become a common experience. Now I had something to bring, and these were surely the people who had the first claim on me for it — not those actual thirty, necessarily (many of whom were scattered over the face of the globe by this time) but as many as possible of these and others like them with whom I had shared common aspirations over the years — to them must I go and say, 'Look what I have found!'

Having made this decision, I received in the post a newsletter from Coombe Springs, and saw in it an S.O.S.: from the beginning of September they would have no cook. I wrote and said that, if it would help to fill a gap, I would come and do this for about a month. My offer was accepted.

It caused great consternation at the office when I gave in my notice, and I was offered a further rise of £200 per annum if I stayed on — apparently no one had noticed I had been doing so little lately. Although there was no reason for it — I intended to use the month at Coombe Springs to get fixed up with a suitable job in the South — a strong feeling came over me that it was the end, not just of a job, but of an era; that I was saying good-bye to the accountancy world for ever. Perhaps it was because, for the first time, I had made a success of this job, and did not have the impulse to 'try again' which a failure engenders, that I now realised this was not where I belonged.

So it was that, a little under three months after I became a Bahá'í, I was to be found boarding the train for London, my flat in an agent's hands for letting, my job a thing of the past.

I do not expect I would have gone back to Coombe Springs if it had been in the same situation as when I had left it two years before. In 1957 Coombe Springs had taken a foster-child — Subud — under its wing, and this foster-child, as it had grown and developed, had very nearly become a cannibal; almost, but not quite, the Coombe Springs we had known before 1957 had been completely 'swallowed up' by it.

But it had not happened like that, and early in 1960 the first step had been taken to establish Subud in the world as a separate entity. In time it would come to have its own independent existence, but the transition was to be a long and painful process which was still, so far, in its early stages. Side by side with this 'weaning' of Subud had come the realisation that the 'foster-mother', who for three years had had all her resources mobilised for this fostering, could begin to have some freedom to fulfil herself in other directions.

Mr Bennett had been the first to look outwards, and had pointed to the constitution of the body which had been formed to own and operate Coombe Springs when the property had been purchased in 1946, and particularly to the first of the Aims and Objects clauses of its Memorandum which established it as a research body. Briefly, this was to promote research into the factors that influence development and regression in the spiritual life of the human race and their operation in individuals and communities, and to study secular and religious theories concerning mankind and our place in the universe. This summed up what Coombe Springs existed for. Fostering Subud had, of course, been in accordance with this, but now it was necessary to look forward.

Strong feelings had been aroused by this attitude. Many people felt that with Subud they had 'got there', that they had come to the end of their search, and that this thing that to them was the final answer was being betrayed by those who thought otherwise. But Mr Bennett would not and could not have suggested that there might be a place at Coombe Springs for interests other than Subud if there had not been a corresponding receptivity among the people. A certain nostalgia for the 'good old days', a feeling that, though Subud provided a valuable element for the inner life, it was only an element — these sentiments had begun to be felt. They were by no means shared by everyone, and the way in which Coombe Springs would return to its purpose of psychokinetic research was obscure. It was at a crossroads, no one could see what the future held for it, or even if it had a future at all.

When I had heard Bahá'ís talking about the difficulties of finding people who would take the Bahá'í Faith seriously, I had felt that I was in a very different position, for I was in contact with many people who were, as I had been, already committed to living their lives according to the Will of God, who would not be blinded by the sort of prejudices the orthodox believer might have — in short, people who would feel the same way as I had done, once they heard. But it was not just the expectation that at Coombe Springs I would find others who might be interested to learn something about the Bahá'í Message that had brought me here; I felt I had to repay a debt. It was thanks to what I had learned here that I had got where I had, and to come back and tell people about it was to lay at their feet in tribute the first fruits of what I had gleaned. As I explained to Mr Bennett, 'I could not just say "I'm all right now" and turn my back on you all.'

The Coombe Springs that I came back to was still a 'Subud place'; it had the same Subud atmosphere, with most of the people who lived there doing so because they wished to share their lives with other Subud members, and such extra-Subud activities as had been initiated played quite a minor part in the lives of most people. But they were beginning to look about a bit, and I did not see why they should not look in the direction of the Bahá'í Faith.

I came to Coombe Springs for a month, and I did — though the process had a feeling of unreality about it — scan the newspapers and apply for some suitable jobs. I think I knew all the time I would stay on, and so it turned out. Over the years I had spent much time assisting in the Coombe Springs kitchen, but to take it over was another matter and I had wondered how I would make out. In the event I surprised myself by the way in which I was able to fulfil the demand of providing a meal for thirty people punctually at 12.45 and 6.30 each day.

As I was managing well, and in any case no one else had been found to replace me, I was asked if I would continue; I agreed, and remained for a further six months. It was hard work, but immensely satisfying — in fact, I look back on this period as one of the happiest of my life. It was a particularly welcome contrast to the job I had just left in Edinburgh, where each client had had, so to speak, his own little cubby-hole in my brain, all filled up with the details of his affairs. Now each day was a day unto itself; at the end of it I had produced good meals or bad meals, but what was done was done and the next day I would start again. My efforts produced immediate results which were, on the whole, appreciated and I was among people by whom I was held in affection and respect.

How pleased I was that, coming back as a Bahá'í, I was here in this capacity of service. The Bahá'í attitude that one's work is a form of worship, which I had found impossible to adopt in my office in Edinburgh, I achieved here in fulfilling the simple and obvious need of feeding people — in the main, that is, for there were times, of course, when it became just a chore. And if anyone had some time to spare to help me peel some apples or cut up some vegetables and if at the same time they wanted to discuss religion, then so much the better.

When I had first heard of the Bahá'í Faith, I had never imagined myself not doing Subud as a result. Subud had been my Way, and I had not been seeking anything to take its place; I had only sought greater understanding. I had found the 'old bottles' of Christianity inappropriate, but had thought I already had the 'new wine' and only needed something to put it in. Only gradually, through association with the Bahá'ís, had I come to realise that these 'new bottles' contained their own 'wine', the quality of which was unsurpassed. The difference between the two kinds of 'wine' was now becoming apparent.

These months afforded me the opportunity to see Subud 'from the outside'. If it had not been for this, there might have been times when it would have seemed attractive to revert to the practice of the *latihan*, where nothing more is required than a 'letting-go'. But now, looking dispassionately at a group of people on whom its action had been operative for four and a half years, I had some misgivings. It was clear to me that it could result in improvements in physical health, release from tensions and greater awareness of spiritual realities, and many people of sound judgment looked upon it as a great gift. One long-standing Subud member, who was a first-class psychiatrist and also a good Christian, and who had had many Subud people in disturbed mental states referred to him, once referred to it as 'this healing force'. However, despite or in addition to these positive aspects, there were some disturbing negative aspects.

Coombe Springs itself showed evidence that this force, which had seemed a stimulant when it swept into our lives in 1957, had now, five years later, revealed itself to be a depressant, just as alcohol is an apparent stimulant but in reality acts as a depressant. The residents showed a marked tendency to develop such characteristics as lethargy, lack of initiative, a passive attitude towards life generally and a certain ultrasensitivity to show themselves. The impression that was left with me as a result of these months of 'looking on' at Subud, was that its practitioners were like greenhouse plants, differing from those that were exposed to the air and the sun as nature intended, growing perhaps faster but less sturdily, and less in accordance with the pattern of their species.

As I said, Coombe Springs was still very much a 'Subud place', and consequently it was a place where anarchy prevailed, each individual finding his highest authority within himself. This was another aspect I was able to 'look on' in these months, and again it was brought home to me — as I had come to suspect more and more during my Subud years at Coombe Springs — that the whole thing was just not practical. To know within oneself what is right is a faculty that should be developed. But in any society or organisation there must be an interplay between this freedom and other, disciplinary, elements if its members are to co-operate together. These were absent here, and many ludicrous situations resulted, as, for instance, when two people were both convinced about the right place in the garden for a certain plant, and the poor thing was moved countless times from the place one knew to be right to the place the other knew to be right and back again!

Subud claims that the practice of the *latihan* is beneficial to the soul. Whether it exerts a beneficial or harmful influence on it, or neither, I do not know. When one considers how many conflicting theories abound as to what is beneficial for the body, how can we imagine we can judge what will benefit our souls? What can one do, then? We are driven back to the fact that there is only one trustworthy source to which one can turn on these matters — the Manifestation of God. Although we may not be able to judge methods for ourselves, it is possible to judge — to rationally weigh up the varied 'evidence' — as to whether the 'credentials' of a Prophet or Revelator are valid. If we are convinced that they are, then we may trust implicitly His Word.

When Pak Subuh visited Coombe Springs in 1959, many people had expressed their eagerness to take more active steps in making Subud better known in the world, but he had discouraged them. The growth of Subud, he had said, depended on God's Will; in God's time and not ours, in His way and not ours, it would expand.

One of the results of the decision to start activities unconnected with Subud at Coombe Springs was that now, on the first Sunday in the month, people came for a day similar to the old 'Coombe Sundays'. This was one such day, and the visitors and residents who were taking part — about thirty all told — were gathered in the upstairs study. Here I had an opportunity of sharing with those present something of what I had experienced over the last few months, and as I did so I learned how, when we align ourselves to God's Purpose, we can become channels for His Power.

I had become a Bahá'í because I had committed myself, in Subud, to living according to the Will of God. It was that decision that had been the turning point of my life, and becoming a Bahá'í the natural result, once I had known about it. When I returned to Coombe Springs I had thought, 'I am no different from anyone else; I just happen to have had an opportunity they have not had'. The reactions I met with, however, forced me to realise that, in the main, I *was* different. 'I don't feel I need a religion', 'Subud gives me all I want' — sentiments such as these were expressed again and again. 'How can you', I thought, 'when faced with the immutability of God's Purpose, talk about what *you* need, what *you* want?'

Anyone who follows a Way based on a particular method runs the risk that the experience will become the aim, and all my training during the years I had been associated with Coombe Springs had taught me to beware of this. In our group we had been told over and over again not to 'work for results'; the various exercises might or might not result in the attainment of certain states, but that was no criterion of their value. The Subud principles of Patience, Submission and Acceptance had also meant carrying on and accepting whatever came or did not come as a result. And yet for many people the aim, I now came to realise, was mysticism for its own sake. We have all experienced moments of spontaneous ecstasy but I have always been convinced that this sort of thing should never be sought, and to spend one's life chasing after it is getting things all the wrong way round. Perhaps this and the prevalent attitude towards sex are symptoms of the same disease, now rife in our society: a lack of wholeness in our lives. Just as sex has its rightful place within the framework of a couple working out their lives together, so union with God has its rightful place within the framework of living as a tool of God. To take either out of context and make the experience an end in itself leads to trouble.

These months at Coombe Springs working in the kitchen had afforded me time to stand back and take stock of myself, to grapple with my new beliefs and begin to work out their implications in my life. And I found I had come to the point of reality where whether one lives or dies are not such terribly important things. I was no longer living — as most of us do — with the knowledge of my mortality pushed into the background. Most important, I now had some identity that existed in its own right in any environment. This had not come about by direct effort alone. For, I now believe, the only way we can see ourselves as one, whole and indivisible, is by seeing ourselves as creatures of God. Surely it is not possible to see ourselves directly. We can see ourselves through the eyes of the world — and the result will be very fragile, which can be easily shattered — or we can see ourselves in the eyes of God — and the result will be whole. I had hesitated in declaring my belief as a Bahá'í because my early training had taught me that it is no small thing to make such a statement as 'I believe'. But I had made it, and it had been valid — it had been the real 'I', my whole being, that had said it, not some ephemeral 'I' that had popped up in me.

This episode had been valuable for me and in many ways I felt reluctant to pass on. But my place did not lie here any longer, though it remained 'home' in the same way the parental home of a married woman, though no longer her place, remains 'home' to her. I prepared to return to the wider world outside the familiar seclusion of Coombe Springs.

My place no longer lay with Subud, but with a company of Bahá'ís who had come to their Faith on many different 'beams'. I had come in on the 'beam' of obedience — if

Bahá'u'lláh's word was the Word of God, then it *must* be obeyed. But there are many other 'beams'. Some have come in on the 'beam' of recognising in the social teachings of Bahá'u'lláh a method of regulating the affairs of mankind which far surpasses any other; a method which does away with the electioneering, the partisanship, the appeal to sectarian interests and the need for the concentration on short-term results of the so-called democracies of the West, at the same time avoiding the dangers of the concentration of power inherent in more dictatorial systems.

Others have come in on the 'beam' of love and others yet because they recognised in the Bahá'í principles — such as the necessity for each person to investigate the truth for himself; the oneness of humanity; the harmony of science and religion; the need for universal education, abandoning of prejudices, a universal language, an international police force; and the rest — that which meets the modern need. There are many ways, and once one has entered, by whatever 'beam', inevitably one finds that here is something with potentialities greater by far than one could ever have imagined.

Not only did I find myself among a company who had come in on different 'beams', I also found that the nature of their entries had varied enormously. Some had bumped in, been catapulted in, and had had their lives turned upside down in the process; others had spent many years in prudent investigation of its tenets, while for some it had been a smooth and gradual metamorphosis.

A deep love between husband and wife may be

prefaced by the most cataclysmic actions of that process known as falling in love, but may equally well come into being so gently that the parties hardly realise what is happening. Neither of these conditions is more likely to produce a happy marriage than the other. Those of the company who had been eased gently in were no less certain.

XVII

AS I LOOK BACK at the events of my 'pre-natal' life, everything seems to have led towards my present position. I had always had a parallel interest in socio-economic systems and methods of inner development, and believed in the need for reform in both the inner life of the individual and the external organisation of society. Neither the one nor the other could by itself result in a world where people lived in a way that was proper to them. I had tended to lose sight of this with the coming of Subud, thinking that *this* was what the world needed. I remember a conversation with a friend in London about Mr Bennett's *Concerning Subud*. We had been talking about the implication in this book that Subud was what was going to save the world. My friend had turned to where Mr Bennett had quoted Albert Schweitzer: 'What that something is, which shall bring new life and new regulative principles to coming centuries, we do not know. We can only dimly divine that it will be the mighty deed of some mighty original genius.'

He had seen the necessity of new life *and* new regulative principles; that they were interdependent and complementary. At the time I had disagreed with my friend's assertion that Subud, which had come without any deed or genius, and had no idea or form, was not what was needed, but the conversation had remained at the back of my mind.

Mr Bennett's influence from 1953 till I left Coombe Springs to go to Edinburgh in 1959 was very potent. The three years he directed us in our study of Gurdjieff's psychological methods gave me something of enduring value, and he eased the mystification when Subud came. By the breadth of his vision — his conception of mankind developing towards maturity by a series of propulsive impulses from a Higher Source — he helped lay the foundation upon which an edifice of understanding was to be built.

The coming of Subud had supplied a missing factor; that God is to be obeyed. The practice of Subud had been a fumbling in the dark to find out what His Will was. I had not known that we also needed to love Him, and in loving Him to love one another — that I found out in the weeks at Kitty's Hut. The 'Kitty's Hut' period helped me to realise that the key lay in discovering the significance of Jesus Christ. When I learned from the Bahá'í teachings that the Manifestations of God — all one, though dwelling amongst us as distinct human entities and called by different names: Abraham, Moses, Jesus, Bahá'u'lláh — are the means by which humanity progresses to the next stage of its evolutionary journey, I knew that at last I held the key.

'Are you aware of it as soon as you wake up in the morning?' Kitty had asked me when I had been a Bahá'í for four or five months. She had hit the nail on the head; that was exactly how it had been then. But the sense of wonder does not continue indefinitely, and after about six months the ecstatic 'honeymoon period' had come to an end. The sense of being 'in the sun', though, is permanent — so long as one keeps oneself spiritually healthy — and I am left with an abiding happiness, even in times of great difficulty and suffering.

It was right that the 'honeymoon period' should have ended when it did; honeymoons are not life, though they may be an essential part of it. Life is not meant to be spent sailing on the crest of a wave, but in a continual working-out. My acceptance of the Bahá'í Faith does not mean the end of my journey. That never ends — one never 'gets there'. Life still consists of a working-out, as it always has. But now the working-out is taking place within a stable framework.

All the elements that I have met with before are there, but they are in their proper place, and in proportion, so I can draw on what my past life has given me. The continual struggle to *be* has proved solid ground-work for the ideal of non-attachment advocated in all sacred literature and with particular stress in the Bahá'í writings. I had become aware of the danger of getting 'lost' in some activity or, as Gurdjieff said, 'disappearing' into it, so that the subject-object relationship is reversed — the machine, the television, or whatever becomes the subject, the human being the object; it has taken over the existence which the human being has lost. I had also become aware of another threat to one's birthright — that of being dominated by the opinions of others. These are things which can become yours for all time.

To find answers to problems 'from within' is a principle that has remained with me, but it is exercised in a more balanced fashion than previously, when I wholeheartedly made Subud my Way. I do not expect to be always relieved of the responsibility of making my own decisions using the ordinary human powers that God has given me. When it comes to decisions in a corporate sense, the Bahá'í Revelation has provided us with institutions and a method of consultation in which both the spark from on high and our own human faculties have their part to play.

I had now got things in focus. I could see that the ferment of the last hundred-and-more years, the result of new modes of thought working themselves out, was caused by the impetus of the Manifestation for this age — Bahá'u'lláh. His coming and the teachings He promulgates are the sowing of the seed; sensitive minds 'pick-up' what is 'in the air', more and more people are influenced, and gradually the world accepts what would formerly have been an anathema. Bahá'u'lláh said that men and women were equal and, half a century later and in another part of the world, the suffragette movement is born. In this sphere, as in so many others, we still have a long way to go before Bahá'u'lláh's principle is fully put into practice, but we are moving towards it.

My friends are aware of an inner change in me and think how nice that I have found something that suits me so well. I find it hard to convey that being a Bahá'í does not just mean following a method which may or may not suit some people. It means participating in a great cosmic Event. We receive spiritual nourishment through the power of the Word, but one cannot regard the Bahá'í Faith only from the point of view of the spiritual growth of the individual, important though this is. One of the exercises advocated by Gurdjieff has been that we should stand and come to an awareness in ourselves: 'Here I am — a man or a woman — standing upright on two legs' and to experience within just what that meant.

To understand the meaning of one's station as a human being and to fulfil it; to understand the stations of other orders of being and to treat them according to their station - that is the key to right living. An animal acts in accordance with its station as an animal and, unlike us, it has no choice but to do so. A human being should be a human being and act in a way becoming to one — which today, by and large, we do not. This much is generally accepted by people of discernment. The Bahá'í teachings tell us also of the next station upwards, the station of Manifestation. Of the essence of these Beings we cannot know because we do not have the capacity to apprehend, but we can look at them and know all that it is possible to know of God.

People drawn to the Bahá'í Faith may enter on the 'beam' of recognition of a perfection which exists nowhere else. Unless they then move forward to appreciate the cosmic role of the Manifestation of God, particularly that of the Manifestation for this age, Bahá'u'lláh, they will miss the point.

The world is sick and Bahá'u'lláh is the Divine

Physician. A sick man may go to a doctor whom he has heard has some miracle-working drug and insist that it be administered to him, but if he is wise he will choose a physician according to his qualifications and reputation and then place himself unreservedly in his hands. He knows the physician has complete understanding of his organism and its condition and will unerringly prescribe the course of treatment suited to it. The harmony of his body will be restored by remedies applied as the wise physician directed.

So it is with the world. When the world places itself unreservedly in the hands of Bahá'u'lláh, then will its sickness be cured.

Glorious and responsible our position is — and exasperating. All around are people trying to find their way through a door to which one has the key; one tries to hold it out to them, but each is looking in his own particular field, and it is too universal for them to accept. In books, in newspapers, on the radio, in ordinary conversation, it is brought home just how different it *could* be, how different it *will* be, when the world has accepted the teachings of Bahá'u'lláh. Parliamentary debates, where the aim is to disparage the opposing political party; proceedings at the United Nations, where each delegate is expected to put his country's interest before that of the world as a whole; the ecumenical movement, where men of goodwill strive for a united Christian church; all demonstrate the need for Bahá'u'lláh's teachings. The world is groping its way towards them and an awareness that our present institutions do not fit the modern need is growing.

Men (and women) within and without these institutions know this and are troubled. *God in my Unbelief*, a book by J.W. Stevenson, the minister of a country parish in Scotland, encapsulates this anxiety. It is in the form of a novel — a novel about a parish such as his own. He is describing two parishioners, each with strongly held, and opposing, political views:

> They came to the House of God, these two, not just differing in politics but doubting each other's integrity; they sat down together to listen to the Word which should have made them one in their common need; and they said together 'Forgive us . . . as we forgive' — and they went out again down the path thinking of each other exactly as they had when they came in and exactly as they had done now for years. There was no meeting-place for them where they could learn to differ with Christian understanding and learn in their differing a greater truth than either had yet seen.
>
> Politics was their point of separation, where they were driven into passing judgement on each other and condemning each other — and yet the issues of politics were the issues of the sharing of God's bread, the caring for the needy, the training of the wrongdoer's evil, the redeeming of the criminal, the setting of the best life before the child. What should have brought them together as Christian men, even with their differences and tensions, was shutting them off

from each other; and just there the Church was doing nothing for them; and the minister was moving with too easy a mind from the one to the other, perhaps a little self-satisfied that he could be a friend to both.

This was where they had to meet, at the point of their difference — not so that one might convert the other to his way of politics but that they might both learn to meet as Christians over the issues of human need, and to differ, if need be, in love. If we could not meet like that we were placing a taboo on politics whenever we were together in Christian circles, deciding to leave the issues of men's common life outside the religion of Christian action; and unreality had at once entered our fellowship. It could not stand the strain; it could continue only by withdrawing from the conflict of ordinary life.

'To meet over the issues of human need' is what Bahá'u'lláh has told us to do. And by putting before us principles of *consultation* outlining the conditions under which 'the clash of differing opinions' may lead to 'the shining spark of truth', He has shown us how it is to be done. 'The war to end war', the First World War was called, but there was a second, and we have been fighting ever since. That war *will* end there can be no doubt. It has been promised all down the ages: by the Old Testament prophets: 'They shall beat their swords into ploughshares and their spears into pruning hooks', and by St John in the Apocalypse: 'And I saw a new heaven and a new earth'. And poets have sung of it, as Tennyson did: 'Till the war-drum throbs no longer, and the battle-flags were furled In the Parliament of man, the Federation of the World' (Locksley Hall).

The prophets could look forward down an immense vista of time; a hundred years ago inspired poets were touched by the vision. As it comes nearer, more and more people sense what will be. I had been struck by one of Mr Bennett's experiences described in his autobiography, *Witness*. He was staying in Macedonia near the Ostrovo swamps, where storks were gathering from all over Europe:

> Early one morning, we heard a great sound, and hastened out of doors to see the entire swamp alive with birds rising. We were to the south of the swamps, which stretched northward for miles. The immense concourse of birds took shape as a great dense column, with single scouts flying at a distance of about a hundred yards from the main body. They flew straight overhead, literally darkening the sky. I tried to count them, but when I reached six hundred I could count no more: the impression was too powerful to be expressed in numbers.
>
> I could not doubt that I was in the presence of an intelligence that operates quite differently from the mind of man. Long after the birds had passed, I remained standing in astonishment. I had become aware of a collective consciousness that remembers and sees and knows the complex pattern of stork life, and yet neither thinks nor expresses itself in words. This collective consciousness must somehow hold, in unity of life and purpose, tens of thousands of

storks, scattered through the summer over the house-tops of Europe. It draws its members together, and for a brief spell the great Stork Being becomes visible as an articulated whole, and then disperses again along the river banks of Egypt and Ethiopia.

We know little of such societies and the collective consciousness in which they share. As I stood in the deep silence left by the great birds, I caught a glimpse of the future of mankind. One day, we shall become aware of the collective consciousness of humanity. It may take millions of years, but when it comes it will be a power incomparably greater than that of any living species. In this vision, there was also a promise that the time was not so far distant when the human race would make a step forward, and begin to look beyond the narrow loyalties of nation, race and religion, towards the distant goal of human unity.

Many men of insight see what is coming, but Bahá'ís believe that the coming of Bahá'u'lláh sowed the seed which may take several hundred years to come to fruition.

When I started life in Edinburgh after two and a half years' intensive Subud experience and looked into the future, I had not been able to discern where the road I was treading was leading. Can I tell where the road I am now treading is leading — subjectively or objectively?

Objectively, I cannot. I have become part of an

embryo-religion: conceived but not yet born. Its potentialities have been delineated, but its mature form is hidden in the future.

Subjectively, I can have more idea. I can look at people on whom this spiritualising power has been operative for two and three generations, and see in many of them a purity I know I can never attain.

An embryo is not a thing of beauty, and the interaction between the energising forces released by Bahá'u'lláh and the body of people who consciously co-operate with them is not something the world can see and admire. But the way a being develops in its embryonic life is of vital importance to its future; at first it may seem to be grotesque, its various parts all out of proportion, but its beauty of form in the life ahead depends on the multiplication and differentiation of its cells in the right way at the right time. So it is with the present development of the Bahá'í Faith. Its adherents are the cells of this embryo-religion, and the fulfilment of its potentialities depends on the right functioning of those cells. It is this which gives significance to our lives.

I do not doubt that there has been a destiny shaping my ends, but strange that I should have come out in the place I least expected — the broad highway of revealed religion, and come into the inheritance of the Christianity I had rejected nearly twenty years before. It is an inheritance belonging in the market place and council chamber, not tamed and shut up in a church, and where 'sociology', 'politics' and 'religion' are swept into one God-facing, God-obeying whole.

ONEWORLD
Books for Thoughtful People

MAIL ORDER

If you would like to receive our mail order catalogue and be placed on our mailing list for regular updates on our current and forthcoming titles, please write to the address below.

Some Oneworld titles you might enjoy are listed here. Please add 15% to cover postage & packing, and send all orders to:

>Oneworld Publications
>185 Banbury Road
>Oxford, OX2 7AR
>England

The Hidden Words
by Bahá'u'lláh

This unusual and inspiring collection of spiritual teachings will appeal to people of all religious persuasions and those who seek a spiritual life. Lucid in style and rich in imagery, these exquisite meditational verses explore the eternal relationship between God and man. Composed by Bahá'u'lláh about the year 1858 whilst exiled to Iraq from his native Persia, *The Hidden Words* is one of the best known and loved of all the author's works.

The book is available in both a cloth gift edition and softcover.

112 pages, cloth £8.95/US$13.95, softcover £3.95/US$6.95

The Prophecies of Jesus
by Michael Sours

In the nineteenth century, many Christians throughout the Western world expected the fulfilment of Jesus's promise to return. This widespread expectation — well documented — culminated in 'The Great Disappointment' of 1844.

The Prophecies of Jesus offers a sensitive, verse-by-verse exploration of Jesus's greatest prophetic sermon, the Olivet Discourse, examines nineteenth century and current Christian interpretations, and presents a lucid analysis in the light of Bahá'u'lláh's teachings.

224 pages, etchings, softcover £10.95/US$18.95

A Study of Bahá'u'lláh's Tablet to the Christians
by Michael Sours

Considered one of the most significant letters of Bahá'u'lláh, founder of the Bahá'í Faith, the Tablet to the Christians presents a penetrating and inspiring message to illumine the path of the sincere seeker. Its passionate and moving appeal, at times reminiscent of the Sermon on the Mount, offers fresh insights into the meaning of a spiritual life and the personal quest for the Kingdom of God.

224 pp, hardcover £12.95/$22.95, softcover £7.95/$13.95

To Understand and Be Understood
by Erik Blumenthal

Erik Blumenthal presents a refreshingly original approach to social life today. Written by an internationally respected psychologist in a warm, anectodal fashion, this book offers down-to-earth, workable advice for successful, loving relationships.

The author brings the reader a new understanding of him or herself and others based on simple, easy-to-use principles, illustrated throughout with real life examples drawn from years of professional practice. A valuable handbook for all those seeking more aware, understanding relationships in all the spheres of their lives.

160 pages, softcover £4.50/US$7.50

Adventures of a World Citizen
by André Brugiroux

This book, now in its fourteenth edition in French, is a humorous and detailed account of the author's eighteen years hitch-hiking around the world. His journey took him through 135 countries and over 250,000 miles. The result is a highly readable travelogue of the 'independent' traveller who eschews the package system and therefore sees more of the true life of the world's people.

Adventures of a World Citizen not only records the physical journey of the author around the world, but also charts his spiritual journey and personal quest for meaning.

288 pages, 12 illustrations, softcover £7.95/US$13.95

Contemplating Life's Greatest Questions

What is the origin of the universe?
Does God Exist?
What is the purpose of life?
Is there a life after death?

These are among the great questions of life, discussed, debated and meditated on throughout humanity's eternal quest for knowledge and understanding. *Contemplating Life's Greatest Questions* explores these and other profound issues in the light of the writings of Bahá'u'lláh, and shares with readers new insights and an inspiring vision of the spiritual life.

96 pages, softcover £4.50/US$7.95

Achieving Peace by the Year 2000
by John Huddleston

If mankind were to decide to establish peace in the world by the year 2000, what practical steps must be taken now - by individuals, politicians, governments and international agencies - in order to achieve this goal? These are the questions addressed in this highly topical book.

Never has peace been so prominent on the international political agenda. In this insightful analysis into the causes of war and barriers to peace, the Chief of the Budget and Planning Division of the IMF examines the psychological, moral and practical issues and puts forward a twelve point plan for establishing world peace.

160 pages, softcover £3.50/US$5.95

The Inner Limits of Mankind
by Ervin Laszlo

This is a spirited and provocative examination of contemporary values and attitudes. A leading systems scientist and philosopher, the author explores ways in which each of us can contribute to their transformation, and argues for the emergence of a new, globally-oriented, environmentally-conscious, spiritually-aware, thinking person.

160 pages, softcover, £4.50/US$7.95